# Maili Chadar, or The Stained Shawl

# AND Truth and Justice

NEW INDIAN PLAYWRIGHTS

# SHANTA GOKHALE

## Maili Chadar, or The Stained Shawl

A TRAGEDY IN FOUR ACTS

## Truth and Justice

FOUR MONOLOGUES

LONDON NEW YORK CALCUTTA

**Seagull Books, 2023**



ISBN 978 1 8030 9 318 5

**British Library Cataloguing-in-Publication Data**
A catalogue record for this book is available from the British Library

Typeset and designed by Seagull Books, Calcutta, India
Printed and bound by Hyam Enterprises, Calcutta, India

# CONTENTS

# Introduction

SHANTA GOKHALE

In 2014, a radical political transformation took place in India. We saw a new kind of politics and a new kind of politician take the stage. A new ideology was promoted and greedily devoured by a large section of the voting public. Democracy was still a necessary word to invoke, but not to adhere to in action.

Those of us who believed that tolerance, respect for all religions and a concern for human rights were the only values that would allow a multicultural society to exist in peace were disturbed at how easily these values were transgressed. The proud claim that a new India was being forged was unfortunately true. It was indeed a new India. Not more evolved, more civilized or more mature, but an India that was encouraged to feel constantly threatened from within by sections of its own citizens; an India that was willing, in the name of security, to be divided and ruled; an India that desperately needed the old colonial law of sedition to keep it safe. Students, journalists, authors and academics were now the enemy, because they thought, argued, questioned and demanded answers. The exercise of democratic rights invited charges of sedition. The new enemy was put behind bars.

How could this happen in a democracy? This was the question that raged in my mind. The only way that I as a writer could address it was through my writing. This much was clear. What was not clear was the form that writing should take. The problem was unexpectedly solved when, on our way home from the theatre one day, my friend Devina asked, 'Can there be a modern tragedy?' I answered without a moment's hesitation, 'Of course there can be. It's happening all around us. Now, here.' There was my answer. I had to write a play. A tragedy.

Even before I knew what I was going to write, I knew what I was not going to write. I was not going to write about the people in power and the dangerous game they were playing. Who were these men and women who filled the pages of our daily newspapers? I knew nothing about them besides their names and faces, how they postured and what they said. I could not see them as human beings living full lives with friends, mothers, husbands, wives and children. The most they could do for me was provide grist for a satire. They were not big enough to make a tragedy. Tragedy was made by multilayered, full-blooded human beings upon whom greatness had been thrust. I wanted to discover in and through the process of writing my play what might happen if such a man were to be my protagonist.

The first thing I had to do, then, was distance myself from the specificities of the present and explore the larger issues that might have led to such a present. I was interested in finding out what human ambition did to human relationships, to the much-vaunted virtues of love and harmony and, ultimately, to man's very humanity. Macbeth stood before me as a towering exemplar, a man of worth who had killed friends, fellow warriors, children, and said callously about his wife's death, 'She should have died hereafter.'

Gradually, my protagonist took shape. With him came those who were near and dear to him. As often happens when you start writing a play or a novel, things you have read, people you have met, songs you have heard begin to gather around your theme like iron filings around a magnet. A bhajan that my mother used to sing, a Verrier Elwin lecture that Shiv Visvanathan had once delivered, the dialogue about truth and justice between Socrates and Thrasymachus that I had read at university, all came back to me unbidden. I made voluminous notes and wrote several key scenes. Soon I came to a point where a beginning had to be made.

I began to write. I made several starts. All false. The material was there. The characters were there. Some events were there. What was not there was the theatrical device, the vessel that would hold everything together and give it shape.

One day I found it. A narrator appeared on my laptop screen. He entered the stage looking over his shoulder and spoke directly to the audience. A narrator is the oldest device in the playwright's book. But a narrator who is also an important player in the action is not. This narrator's very first actions and words told me he was going to be both narrator and character. All I had to do now was to trust him and let him take the play forward. He took instant charge. He put the scenes I had written into a new order and led me to write others. Writing the play was now a matter of time and writerly skill, followed by editing, rewriting and tightening till the play was of a shape, style and substance that satisfied me.

Four years had passed since my brief conversation with Devina. The play it triggered was now done. *Maili Chadar, or The Stained Shawl: A Tragedy in Four Acts.*

*

For many years now, it has been my practice to save material that might serve as a source for a play. In 2002, after the communal riots in Gujarat, I began saving everything related to the burning of Best Bakery. Of all the horrendous crimes that had been committed during those days, the

Best Bakery tragedy haunted me because of the human story I saw at its centre. Zaheera Sheikh, the 16-year-old survivor of the inferno, had become the star witness of the case. Before she knew it, she was jettisoned into a legal web that she could neither understand nor escape. Initially, I wanted to write a full-length play about her predicament. I made many starts but lost my way each time in the jungle of details I had collected, the number of people and agencies involved and the moral and legal complexities the case threw up. Eventually, it became clear to me that I was too close to the events to make sense of them. I gave up. However, Zaheera stayed with me as an unfinished project.

One day, quite unexpectedly, almost two decades after the Gujarat riots, I saw light. I saw that a monologue would allow me to concentrate exclusively on the questions that had most concerned me during Zaheera's trials—questions about truth and justice. Zaheera had been convicted of perjury and imprisoned in Byculla Jail for a year. As far as the outside world was concerned, 'justice had taken its course' and she could be forgotten. But I began to wonder what she thought about during that year of incarceration, about herself and about society and the law as she had experienced it all between her years of innocence and the events that had turned her, the victim, into a 'criminal'. No details of her life in jail had been investigated by any journalist as far as I knew. The field was wide open for me to imagine and reconstruct her thoughts. The Zaheera monologue is thus a piece of pure fiction based on fact.

When I finished writing this monologue, two possible companion monologues suggested themselves to me. Saved in my folder were Emile Zola's letter 'J'accuse' about the Dreyfus Affair that had shaken nineteenth-century Paris; and the article that Sri Lankan editor Lasantha Wickrematunge had written in anticipation of his assassination, which he had foretold would happen in retribution of his opposition to his government's murderous policies against a minority community.

The Dreyfus monologue had to be spoken by Lucie Dreyfus who had outlived Alfred Dreyfus by 40 years and was known to have never forgiven France for what it had done to him. I saw love and bitterness there. I saw her looking back on events that still made her blood boil because of their sheer injustice and the falsehoods on which they were based. As I worked on my ideas, another facet of the case began to intrigue me: the role that an unknown charwoman had played in providing the only 'evidence' the French military possessed against Dreyfus. No details were available about her, not even her name. I was free to invent her character from scratch, which I did, complete with husband and children. Her short monologue precedes Lucie's.

Wickrematunge's powerful article was itself a monologue of sorts; but it was not written for the stage. At the time when I was mulling over a monologue using his article, the press in India had allowed itself to be gagged by a government that could not stomach questions. Media owners were showing the door to journalists who did not wish to be turned into lapdogs. Wickrematunge's article was relevant to this situation in every way. I decided to make it the context of a monologue spoken by an invented character who could represent the numerous journalists who had abandoned the mainstream press for the internet where they were free to practise their profession. Wickrematunge's article served as the lodestar in her monologue.

# MAILI CHADAR, OR THE STAINED SHAWL

*A Tragedy in Four Acts*

*For Devina*
who once asked, 'Can there be a modern tragedy?'

CHARACTERS

PEON: narrator and character

JEET: Aged 20 to 40

KARAN: Aged 20 to 40

SHARMISHTHA: Aged 20 to 40

PRINCE: Aged 20 to 40

MA: Aged 60 to 80

GREAT-GRANDPA: Indeterminate age

THADANI, OAK, PATEL:

Aged 60 to 80 as TOP officials

40 as businessmen/industrialists

40 as policemen

40 as priests

No special set required. Props as suggested

TIME SPAN

20 years

*The stage is dark. Peon enters front stage, looking cautiously over his shoulders. He is wearing an extravagantly colourful shirt.*

PEON. Yes, well, you have to be careful. I don't mean you. I mean I. And people like me. PLMs. You are probably more familiar with PLUs, the chatterati. PLMs can't afford to chat. Mouths shut except to yawn or shove in food. We are those who must be present but look absent. We are those who have names but must not expect to be called by them. We are those who have legs but must move only when the boss says so. We are the peons of the world. There are other names for us. Gopher. Flunkey. Minion. When you're blessed with democratic bosses, you're Office Attendant. Or even Office Assistant. Then there are names we call ourselves when we're pissed off. Drudge! Slave! Scum!

I don't. It's to do with how you look at life. I learned about SWOT in my first job. The word was bandied about a lot in that office. I gathered it was a way to assess how you stood in any given situation. Strengths, Weaknesses, Opportunities, Threats. So in my spare time, I've jotted down my SWOT analysis:

Strength: My ability to be present but look absent

Weakness: Traces of ego arising from the entirely mistaken notion that I am a human being, and not a piece of furniture.

Threat: The possibility of my boss noticing me and taking umbrage.

Opportunity: Being a fly on the wall, listening and learning.

You might wonder how with this rather conspicuous body I can make myself invisible. It's like this. Over time, you learn there's a difference between being there and being noticed. Once SWOT tells you that your strength lies in not being noticed, then do what I do.

Don't wear colour. Don't eat garlic. Shrink into yourself and assume a non-threatening look. I worked hard on mine in my first job. Just let your mouth hang open a little. Like this. Take care not to overdo it. Otherwise you'll look like a moron and the boss won't entrust Top Secret files to you. Just a little. Like this. Look like a simple old soul everybody can trust. I've taken my cue from Hamlet: 'Let your own discretion be your tutor'. How do I know Hamlet? Ah. That's something you'll gather by and by. We narrators can't let out all our secrets at one go, can we?

So let's get down to business. Introductions. I've stolen the idea from *Antigone*. No, not Sophocles. Anouilh: 'Well here we are. These people are about to act out for you the story of Antigone.' So here we are . . .

(*He turns. The stage lights up gradually, revealing three men sitting at a large desk stage right; three men in varicoloured chairs centre stage; an old woman on a string cot stage left; a young woman behind bars upstage centre. Behind her, in semi-darkness, a very, very old man.*)

These people are about to present before you *Maili Chadar, or The Stained Shawl: A Tragedy in Four Acts.*

(*The old woman sits up slowly and sings 'Maili chadar odh ke kaise / Dwar tumhare aaun / He paavan parameshvar mere / man hi man sharmaaun'. Lies down again. Silence*)

Sorry. That was out of turn. I meant to start from the right. So that there is Mr Harish Patel. That's Mr Sudarshan Oak. And that's Mr Indru Thadani. Thadani is T, Oak is O, Patel is P—TOP. Their organization. They also call themselves the Pathfinders. They are my bosses. I am their drudge.

Moving over, the man in the red chair is Jeet. I shall not divulge his surname. I don't want any community or caste group threatening to rape my mother. Although she's dead. My mother. Died of starvation five years ago.





The man in the grey chair is Karan. No surname. Reason? Same as above. He and Jeet are college chums. Same class. Same interests. Acted in plays. Wrote poetry. Sang and what not. Karan lost his parents in an accident. Jeet's parents adopted him. So they are half-brothers in a way.

On the yellow chair is Prince. I'm not joking. That's his given name. Patel says he's his nephew. But others say (*looks over his shoulder and drops his voice to a whisper*) he's his love child. (*Winks*) Just look at Patel. Would you believe it?

Moving left, that's Jeet's mother. A widow. Everybody calls her Ma. Her husband was called Baba. She has a few health issues. But she's tough.

The young woman behind bars is Sharmishtha, Jeet's sweetheart since college.

Beyond her in the shadows is my great grandfather. Tough old man and stubborn as hell. I am forty. So he must be at least a hundred.

There you are. The story begins about twenty years ago. Jeet has just won the Young Leader Crown, and Karan, the Promising Young Leader Pugdee in TOP's Leadership Quest. Prince has won an honourable mention. Sharmishtha and the other finalist have won nothing. She is not much of a poet. But she has opinions. Worse, she has convictions. (*Exit*)

*Darkness.*

## ACT 1

### Scene 1

*Lights come up. Thadani, Oak, Patel are seated around the table. Peon brings in a tray of tea and pours it out for them. He is wearing a nondescript pant and shirt and his mouth-half-open expression. Tea and biscuits served, he retreats to a stool in a far corner of the room.*

OAK (*sipping tea*). Did you see what I saw yesterday?

PATEL. Not likely. Your eyes are made to see a single grain of dust in a whirlwind.

THADANI. The poetry bug's caught him.

OAK. Oh, come on Patel. It's not eyes—it's observation.

THADANI. I think I saw what you saw.

OAK. Then kindly clear the dust from our friend's eyes.

THADANI. Why? You do it.

OAK. Did you not see a particular closeness between two of our finalists?

PATEL. Yes, yes. Jeet and Karan. Very unnatural. That man Karan is dangerous.

OAK. Jeet and Sharmishtha, Patel. Jeet and Sharmishtha. If we are planning anything with him, we'll have to watch her, not Karan. He's harmless.

PATEL. He is not. But if anyone needs watching, it's our man himself. Jeet. I distrust men who write poetry—I'm a man of action.

THADANI. Let's refine your idea of yourself, Patel. Let us say you are a man of commercial action.

PATEL. And proud of it.

THADANI. But Oak, Karan might be more harmful than you think. His poem about the two sides of patriotism was dangerous. A man who sees both sides of things doesn't move and won't let others move either. There should be no hair-splitting with patriotism. It is what it is. The noblest emotion the human heart is capable of. Jeet's poem was passionate. It showed a single-minded vision.

PATEL. Don't look at me. I've told you what I think of men who write poetry. I was against the poetry round from the start. Prince did the right thing. Went to Google, typed in 'patriot' and picked the poem that popped up first.

OAK. Which happened to be the most famous—Robert Browning's—and as bad as Karan's in what it said.

PATEL. But it wasn't what he thought. It was what Browning thought. And that shouldn't matter to us

THADANI. I don't think he even knew what it said. Yes, it was a damaging poem. First this man is hailed as a patriot, and then he is stoned. Why? The poem doesn't tell you. It was rubbish!

OAK. Now listen to Jeet's poem. (*Plays a video cassette.*)

*Projection on cyclorama. Jeet reads with controlled emotion.*

JEET. 'Towards the Dawn'

It was by sheerest chance they met,
The bright-eyed youth, the blind-eyed seer.
The youth much pained said, 'Revered sir,
Can you foretell what lies ahead?

'For in this place and in these times
I see such misery, such ceaseless tears.
The parched earth cries for succour here
And people live in endless fear.

'In times gone by, the gods came down,
Destroyed our enemies one by one
With clever craft and magic might,
Wielding weapons forged in heaven.

'Will neither god nor goddess come
To save us in this dark, drear age?

Will no avatar take human form?
Please answer me, oh venerable sage.'

The sage said with a sigh profound,
'The future, sadly, I cannot tell.
The here and now is all I see—
I see what is, not what will be.

'I see amongst us fine, brave men,
Strong of mind, with nerves of steel.
Patriots every one of them who,
Still unknown, will die unseen.

'But from among them might arise
A leader of courage and iron will
With power to force the darkness out
And bring our lost light flooding in.

'Young men of faith and eager brawn
Will be his mighty army then.
They'll fight with him to save our land
From present grief and future pain.'

The young man looking up ahead
Saw dawn break through the pall of night.
His muscles taut, his head raised high
He felt the sun rise in his breast.

*Loud applause. View of young audience applauding and Jeet folding his hands in acknowledgement.*

OAK. It's given me goosebumps again. Did you see how his chest expanded when he recited it? Didn't once glance at the paper in his hand. Knew it off by heart. He saw himself as the young man. That's exactly the vision we are looking for. He is our man. Come on.

PATEL (*sighs*). I don't think so. But since you're so sure, I'll go along with you. But please note. With reservations about men who write poetry.

THADANI. Noted. So now you're with us? (*Patel nods.*) Then we'll send him the letter? (*Patel nods again. Thadani draws a letter from a file, folds it and puts it in an envelope. Looks at Peon.*) What's his name?

OAK. Whose?

THADANI. Our man.

PATEL. Just clap and he'll come.

*Thadani claps. Peon hurries forward.*

OAK. Give. To Jeet. Home. Jeet. Understand? (*Peon nods, takes the letter and leaves*) You never know whether he's heard. And if he has, whether he's understood.

PATEL. Well. You were the one who wanted to engage an Vanvasi. That's what he is.

THADANI. I did too. This place is full of them. Aren't we looking for ways to take this whole region forward?

*Patel shrugs noncommittally. Oak and Thadani exchange looks.*

PATEL. I'm not for mixing charity with business.

OAK. This isn't charity, Patel. It's pragmatism. Strategy. And it's certainly not business. We're building a nation.

THADANI. Look, let's not get into that old wrangle. Our agreement is that we hang together for ten years. If the result is zero, we split.

## Scene 2

*The TOP trio on one side of the desk. Jeet enters.*

THADANI. Jay Shri Krishna. Please sit.

OAK. That was a very fine poem you recited. Very fine.

JEET. Thank you, sir.

PATEL. Do you write a lot of poetry?

JEET. Not a lot. Some. But I read a lot. We have a poetry circle.

THADANI. Tagore?

JEET. And Nirala, Muktibodh, Surve, Neruda, Yeats . . . and our own—

THADANI. You know all those languages?

JEET (*laughs, shakes his head*). Wish I did. No. In English translation.

OAK. Will you have some tea?

JEET. No, thank you. Just had some.

OAK. I suppose you're wondering why we've asked you to come here today. Let me get to the point straightaway. We have watched you from the time you were at college.

JEET. Excuse me?

THADANI. My colleague said we have watched you since you were at college.

JEET. You mean you? I never saw you.

PATEL. We will count that as our success.

THADANI. We saw you in the agitation against the professor who misbehaved with a girl.

JEET. Molested.

THADANI. That's what I mean. And you made a fiery speech. You have a way with words. You captivated the students.

JEET. The words came from my heart.

THADANI. Sure, sure. Let us say your heart is in the right place.

OAK. We are looking for young men like you. Educated, principled, courageous. Your poem hit the nail. You are right. We cannot wait for a saviour. We must help ourselves. By we, I don't mean us greyheads. We is you. The young.

*Long pause.*

THADANI. We have an offer for you. We belong to a very large organization. The Pathfinders. The three of us form one of its subsidiaries—TOP. Thadani, Oak, Patel. (*Sheepish laughter*) The Pathfinders run a leadership programme. We would like to sponsor you for it. Would you like that?

JEET (*wary*). What kind of leadership?

OAK. Just leadership. It could even be political leadership.

PATEL. I see you wrinkle your nose. Why?

JEET. My father always said: If you want to do good work, stay out of politics. I didn't even stand for student elections.

THADANI. Don't we know that? Isn't that why we've asked you to meet us? There can be a politics that's very different from the kind your father detested. And quite rightly too.

JEET. I don't know about that. I wouldn't like to let him down. He always quoted Hamlet to me: 'This above all: to thine own self be true, And it must follow, as the night the day, Thou canst not then be false to any man.'

OAK. Your father was a learned man, and a good man, and we respected him deeply. He could have minted money. But he chose not to. We value you because you are his son. If you want to carry forward his legacy, you can't do it by trying to be him.

PATEL. Look around you, son. Is the world you see the same as the world your father left when he passed away?

JEET. No.

PATEL. Are you a doctor like your father?

JEET. No.

PATEL. So what profession will you practise? How will you serve our people as your father did?

OAK. How will you carry forward your father's work with philosophy and literature? With your courage and vision. Let our land benefit by it. It needs clean, selfless men. We aren't talking about politics for personal power. It should never be for personal power. As your father's son, we believe you are free of personal ambition. As your father's son, we also know that selfless service is in your DNA.

THADANI. Think over it. The leadership course is for one year. We charge nothing. The best minds in the country talk to you. Yes, talk. Not lecture. If at the end of it, you feel you have gained nothing, our dialogue will end. You can move on. Follow your own path.

PATEL. So? Will you give it a thought?

THADANI. Will you?

JEET. Maybe. Let me speak to my mother and friends.

OAK. Are you not your own man? Do you always discuss your plans with your mother and friends?

JEET (*looking them in the eye*). Mother most certainly. Friends, a lot of the times. Close friends.

OAK. Like Karan. And Sharmishtha. Are you—is she . . .

THADANI. Oak belongs to the old school. There are things he cannot bring himself to say.

OAK. Nonsense.

THADANI. Then say it.

OAK (*softly*). I didn't want to because it's personal. But yes, we need to know. Are you and Sharmishtha in love?

JEET (*blushing*). We hope to marry one day.

PATEL. Congratulations. That's wonderful news.

THADANI. Congratulations to you too, Oak, for uttering that four-letter word.

*They all laugh including Jeet. Then Jeet stands up.*

JEET. May I go now?

THADANI. Yes, of course. Let us know your decision.

OAK. Meanwhile, keep writing. You might turn out to be a good poet. Despite what Plato said, we need poets in our state.

*Jeet rises, folds his hands, his back erect, his face aglow with a smile. He is about to leave when Thadani claps, and Peon hastens forward, holding out a packet.*

THADANI. Something that will tell you about the Pathfinders. And us.

*Jeet leaves, holding the packet rather gingerly.*

OAK. Do you see a soft vein there in which we might inject something harder like ambition?

PATEL. Yes. He hasn't even asked himself what he wants to do. I can't believe it. From the day I was born, I knew what I wanted to do.

THADANI. Let me guess. Make money?

PATEL. Yes. Has either of you ever met a poor Patel?

*Laughter. Lights fade.*

**Scene 3**

*A dimly lit room. A chatai on the floor. A cot on which Ma is resting. Behind her on the wall, two photographs. One of Gandhi. The other of a small group of Adivasi men and women and an elderly man in a pajama-kurta. Jeet sits on the chatai.*

MA. How long will you be gone?

JEET. I didn't say I was going, Ma.

MA. How long did they say you'll have to be away?

JEET. A year.

MA. Where?

JEET. I didn't ask

MA. Do you want to go?

JEET. I don't know. It might be worth trying. I'm not doing anything else.

MA. Your father's work is short of hands.

JEET. Father had a private practice to live off. I don't.

MA. You will. You've only just got your degree.

JEET (*doubtfully*). In literature and philosophy.

MA. You chose the subjects. You can teach. And work here.

JEET. I've thought about that, Ma. I'm not sure I could live the way you and Baba did. You were practising what you had been trained for. Medicine. Sharmishtha teaches the children. What will I do?

MA. Help her teach the children. There are more tribals in need of education than she can teach in seven lifetimes.

JEET. But don't you think training for politics would allow me to help them more? Schools, well-equipped medical centres, jobs . . .

MA (*sighs*). I can see you want to go. Your father and I have never stood between you and your wishes. What about Sharmishtha?

JEET. I'm coming back in a year, Ma. We weren't planning to marry so soon anyway.

MA. I need to know where she will fit into your plans. She may not want a politician husband.

JEET. One step at a time, Ma. We're talking about a year's training. And you've already made me a politician. (*Pause*) I'll talk to her. Don't worry. I'll do the honourable thing. Will you bless me, please?

MA. Do what your heart tells you. Remember what Baba always said.

JEET. To thine own self be true. Trust me, Ma.

*He bends over her feet. A long pause while various emotions flit over her face. Then she blesses him.*

**Scene 4**

*Sharmishtha and Jeet are seated on a bench, silent. She looks upset.*

JEET (*breaking the silence*). It's only for a year, love.

SHARMISHTHA. Who are these men?

JEET. You saw them every day during the competition. They spoke to us. Looked after us. They are good men.

SHARMISHTHA. It's creepy to think they kept tabs on us in college. You're a natural leader, Jeet. You don't need training in leadership.

JEET. You do if it is political leadership.

SHARMISHTHA. What about Baba's warning . . .

JEET. I shall remember it every day while I'm away. If this leadership thing provides a way to be of service to my people, I have my future made. I shall prove that politics doesn't make us—we make politics. I shall prove that politics can help the poor much more than one lone doctor and one lone teacher working with one lone group of Adivasis.

SHARMISHTHA. I can see that your mind is made up.

JEET. It wasn't until I began to defend the idea with Ma and now with you. In settling your doubts, I have settled mine.

SHARMISHTHA. So you will say yes to those men?

JEET. Not yet. I'll talk to Karan.

SHARMISHTHA. Again?

JEET. Last time he wasn't sure. He said he'd think about it.

SHARMISHTHA. He'll see both sides of the issue. He'll see why Ma and I have grave doubts. And then he'll see why you want to go. Fat use that's going to be.

JEET. You misjudge him.

SHARMISHTHA. Take my advice. Don't ask him what you should do. Simply tell him you are going.

JEET. You're harsh.

SHARMISHTHA. I'm worried, Jeet. You're going to lose your independence chasing a chimera.

JEET. It's not a chimera. Those men know what they're talking about. They've assured me that, after the course, I'm free to decide what I want to do.

SHARMISHTHA. They've caught you at a vulnerable point. Clever. Like spiders waiting for their prey . . .

JEET (*laughs out loud*). I understand where that is coming from. I understand your concern. Your concern will be my guiding light . . .

SHARMISHTHA (*interrupts, and stands up*). You know I hate mush. Do me a favour, Jeet. Don't come to say goodbye when you leave. I'm not sure I'll take it well. (*Begins to walk away. Jeet grabs her hand and pulls her close. She lays her head on his chest for a moment*) I'll say goodbye now. I hope you're doing the right thing. Good luck.

*Jeet looks after her, pained. Karan enters from the other side and sits down in Sharmishtha's place.*

KARAN. What did she say?

JEET. Good luck.

KARAN. Oh. And Ma?

JEET. 'Remember what Baba always said.'

KARAN. And you?

JEET. I'll think about it.

KARAN. I've thought about it.

JEET. And?

KARAN. I haven't changed my mind. I don't think you should . . .

JEET. Go? And do what instead?

KARAN. You'd decided to do your MA.

JEET. And then a PhD? Like you?

KARAN. Why not?

JEET. And then? Teach?

KARAN. People do. I'm going to. That's also service. Opening up young people's minds.

JEET. Was that done for us?

KARAN. Something was done. Or happened. Nobody stopped us from reading. And thinking. We can do better. We will do what wasn't done for us. We will excite young minds with ideas. Imagine, Jeet, you in literature and I in philosophy. What worlds of wonderment we will open up for them . . .

JEET. You are living in a bubble. Who opts for literature and philosophy these days? Those who can't get through to anything else.

KARAN. Is that why we did? If we can spark even one young mind . . .

JEET. No, Karan. (*Rises. So does Karan. Jeet puts his hands on Karan's shoulder. Then turns around and begins to walk towards the exit, his arm still around Karan's shoulder.*) I wish the idea of teaching could excite me as much as it does you. You make it sound magical. All I can see is stupid faces, half asleep, rushing to their guide books before the exams . . .

*They walk out together. Enter Peon from the other wing, in a yellow kurta, white pajama and a checked gamchha round his neck.*

PEON. Surprise, surprise! The theatre company's wardrobe man said: Wear this. I wore it. Ours not to question why. Ours but to do and die. The dying will come later. Meanwhile, there's a reason why I'm tricked out like this. I'm going North. I'm told Northerners wear this kind of thing. Why North? Because Jeet is going North. Into the mountains. Yes, he has decided. He had to. He kept dithering. He stopped talking to Ma, Karan, Sharmishtha. He began taking long walks through the forest, up the hill, along the river. Sitting under the trees.

Gazing into the sky. In the heat of day. In the cool of night. Those were hectic days for me. I was his invisible shadow. Bosses' orders. I woke when he woke. I slept when he slept. I was given this phone. A new contraption. No wires. See? With this I could speak to the bosses. He's sitting under a tree, I'd tell them. He's reading something, I'd tell them. What is he reading, they'd ask. I can't tell from this distance, I'd say. Then the shadow play ended. The battle began face-to-face. I was sent to hunt him down. With messages. Letters. Oak and Thadani were sweating. Patel was gloating. He said nothing, but his face said: I told you so. Jeet's responses were always the same: I need time to think. The bosses' last message was: there is no time to think. Unless we book your place in the course, NOW, you will lose your chance. Jeet sighed a big sigh. Got up. Squared his shoulders and said: tell them to book my seat.

So we're off to the mountains. To my mind, leadership should be taught as close to the ground as possible. But big men know better. So northwards we will go—Jeet, and I as a spy, pretending to be his factotum. My bosses say they are 'developing' me. Giving me chances. I would never have gone, otherwise. It's noble of them. Pick something out of the dirt and develop it for its own good. The dirt is too dumb to know what's good for it. Spying and writing reports is good for me. (*Pulls out a sheet of paper from his pocket.*) This is called a proforma. I am carrying a bagful of them. One for every day of the year. It has columns for things like: 'Classroom Attendance', 'Time in Library', 'Time Chatting with Batchmates', 'Time at Yoga'. The last column is for 'Anything Unusual'. That's my real test. I mean, what's unusual? Sneezed in the morning? Spent too long on the pot? Looked too happy? Looked too glum? I am also to report on how many letters he writes to Sharmishtha and how many he gets in return. Letters from Ma and Karan don't matter.

(*Does a little song and dance*)

We are going to the mountains, want to come?
We are going to the mountains, want to come?
We are going to the mountains,
We are going to the mountains,
We are going to the mountains, oh what fun.

I'll miss my Sundays off. Going back to the pada. Sitting with Great-grandpa. And the trees. The trees. (*Looks morose. Walks slowly away with many backward looks and a sad wave of the hand.*)

*Darkness.*

**Scene 5**

*The TOP office. Oak and Thadani are pacing the floor. Patel is on the phone.*

PATEL. I told you a million times, don't trust. In business there is no trust. Trust only yourself. Not even a blood brother. Hope you've learnt your lesson now. Stop listening to that woman. She doesn't understand business. Is that clear, son? Good. (*The other two look questioningly at him as he puts down his cell phone*) Ajay. My son. Hasn't yet learnt. I'm beginning to think he never will. Prince has it in his blood. This chap . . . ? (*Shrugs*) See . . . we grow up, our families think it's time to marry him off. They get you a girl. You marry her. She's from a business family. Her father has so much money doesn't know what to do with it. Your parents think it's a perfect match. You think so too. Speaks your language, cooks your food yes. BUT DOESN'T UNDERSTAND BUSINESS. That's OK. She doesn't. She's not going to be a partner in the company anyway. Just for the sake of it she's on the Board of Directors. But then she goes and passes on her genes to the son.

THADANI. It's not a deliberate act, Patel.

PATEL. Deliberate or not . . . and I'm not saying my parents should have seen her gene chart along with her kundali—I'm saying, this is what has happened. I've done my best for the child. But when I put him through the test that my father put me through, I knew what to expect. (*Gets up and starts pacing the floor.*)

*Oak and Thadani sit down.*

OAK. Calm down, Patel. He'll be fine I'm sure.

THADANI. What test?

PATEL. What?

THADANI. The test your father . . .

PATEL. Yes, yes, that. It's a family test. An heirloom, you can say. Handed down from father to son. (*Stops pacing. Stands, thinking.*)

THADANI. We're waiting, Patel.

PATEL. Ah yes. Your son is five years old. You stand him on a table. You say, Jump. Naturally he's afraid. You say: Nothing will happen. Jump. I'll hold you. You spread out your arms. Just as the child jumps, you move away. The child falls and learns his lesson: Don't trust even your father.

OAK. That's brutal.

PATEL. Business is brutal. I didn't jump. I sat down on the table and then climbed down on my own. My father was proud of me. But this fellow. My son. He grins at me like a jackass, and jumps. When he falls, he doesn't know why I didn't catch him. He bawls and runs to his mother who makes big eyes at me. (*Starts to pace again.*) That's why I wasn't keen on this fellow, Jeet. Both his parents' genes are in him. Writes poetry. Humph! Where is he now? Hunh? Where is he? And that Vanvasi of yours? Bolted, both of them.

OAK. They're only a day late.

PATEL. What does that mean? Is that leadership? Leadership is discipline, punctuality, responsibility.

THADANI. We're not talking social leadership here—we're talking political leadership. That involves slyness, bending rules, making the false sound true.

PATEL. Out there. Out there. Not here with his benefactors. And we haven't made him a political leader yet. Or have we? Have you two been . . . behind my back . . .

OAK. Would we do that? You should trust us, Patel.

THADANI. We are not in a business partnership. This is different. You must trust us.

*Long silence. All three are sunk in their own thoughts. They don't notice Peon's presence till he clears his throat. He is wearing his usual pant-shirt. They look at him blankly, not reacting. Then*:

ALL THREE (*at once*). What the . . . Where have you . . . Where is . . .

PEON. I don't know.

OAK. Don't know? Don't know what?

PEON. Where he is.

THADANI. How can you not know? Your tickets were booked together. Your seats were side by side. You were with him the night before you left. Your report said so. Then?

PEON. I wrote the report and slept. I had packed our things. We were ready to go. I got up at 5 in the morning. The train was leaving at 8. We had to . . . do 'those things'—have bath, eat breakfast—and leave at 7. I wanted to go to the bathroom. The door was shut. I looked at his bed. He wasn't there. He must have got up before me, I thought. No problem, I thought. He doesn't take long, I thought. Five minutes on the . . .

PATEL. Yes, yes. No shitty details . . .

THADANI. Patel!

OAK. Yes, yes, go on.

PEON. He's quick is all I'm saying. Ten minutes for everything. But fifteen minutes and he still hadn't come out. I knocked on the bathroom door. Nothing. Knocked harder. Nothing. Pushed. It opened.

THADANI. Opened?

PEON. And he wasn't there.

PATEL. You mean, he was never there? (*Peon nods.*) You idiot! Why did you think he was?

PEON. Where else in the morning?

THADANI. But didn't you suspect?

PEON. How?

PATEL. Bathroom sounds, idiot. Natural human sounds.

PEON. He never made any. Real gentleman.

*They look at him, their mouths open*

ALL THREE. So?

PEON. So I knocked on his friends' doors. It was a big house. Took me time to do the rounds. Everybody was packing. Still, they wanted to know what had happened. They heard he was missing. They said: Really? He's not there? (*Long pause*) That's how I missed my train. Next train: two days later.

THADANI. I suppose you paid for your ticket. (*Puts his hand in his pocket and takes out his wallet.*)

PATEL. No need. He must have travelled ticketless. These people do it all the time.

*Peon pulls out a piece of paper from his pocket and places it on the table. Thadani looks at it, gives Patel an amused look and holds out the fare. Nobody says anything.*

OAK. Well . . . what can we say? He's not to blame.

PATEL. Of course he is. We won't pay him.

OAK. We can't do that, Patel. He did his duty. He's only a simple uneducated . . .

PEON. Twelfth pass, sir . . .

OAK. What?

PEON. I've done my twelfth. Passed.

PATEL. Oh, really?

THADANI. That's why we hired him, gentlemen.

OAK. True. True. Anyway, what I meant was that a simple man like him is no match for Jeet.

PEON. He got the best grade, sir. Top of the class.

THADANI. We know that. The organizers sent us the results. (*Pause*) Would you like to take a couple of days off? You must be tired.

PEON. That would be nice. Really nice. Thank you, sir. Thank you. Thank you. (*Exit*)

OAK. So? Now what?

PATEL. Prince has come back.

THADANI. Oh? Did he go?

PATEL. Of course he went. He's a sharp young man.

OAK. But we didn't—

PATEL. Sponsor him? Of course we didn't. Why would he need our sponsorship? There's money spilling out of his father's pockets.

THADANI. The Pathfinders ask for more than money. Recommendation.

PATEL (*laughs out loud, pointing derisively at Oak*). Money is its own recommendation, Oak.

OAK. Not with the Pathfinders. Money can't buy them.

THADANI. Oak, I think you . . .

PATEL. OK. Then you tell me how Prince got his seat in the course.

*Oak looks at Patel and then at Thadani, both stone-faced.*

*Blackout.*

**Scene 6**

*Under a tree in Peon's village.*

GREAT-GRANDPA. Let me begin at the beginning.

PEON. How long ago would that be?

GREAT-GRANDPA. That would be when all the land of this earth was joined together and so also the seas. The earth was thick with trees. Birds nested in them, tigers and elephants roamed under them and we ate their roots, leaves and fruits. Then came the great upheaval. The earth moved, mountains rose, rivers were formed. The seas flooded into the creeks. And the earth moved again. Parts of it drifted away. One piece went north. One piece went south. One piece went east and one piece went west. For many years, the birds flew scared and the animals did not know where to go. The only creatures neither afraid nor confused were the snakes and earthworms who still had their earth. Suddenly, two unknown men came from an unknown part of the land and said: we are here to burn down the forest. They did not look like us nor speak like us. Why will you burn the forest, we asked. Because you have sheltered the snakes, they said. They were very angry with the snakes. To kill them, they burned down the whole forest.

PEON. 'And when they were done, / not one green leaf, / not a single blade of grass / was left behind. Just miles of ash that kept smouldering / for months afterwards.'

GREAT-GRANDPA. How do you know?

PEON. I don't know. The poet knows.

GREAT-GRANDPA. I suppose that is what happened. But we had fled. Over hills, into deserts, across rivers and finally into a forest far away, yearning for our own. We kept returning, kept returning, kept returning. And soon we found that the deep roots of our forest had begun to put out shoots. And the river still flowed. One by one, we returned to our land. It was a miracle to behold as tender shoots turned into saplings and saplings into trees. Our tribe's woes were over. The forest was back as it was before. The birds returned to nest in its trees, and the animals came back to wander in the shade. And our people had roots and leaves and fruit to fill them and more.

PEON (*glancing at his watch*). How much longer will your story take, Great-grandpa?

GREAT-GRANDPA. It will take as long as it takes. I will tell you now about an old man who lived among us. A great-grandfather. He said to the young men and women of the tribe: we should not have let the unknown men burn down our forest. We will not let that happen again. I want you to pledge yourselves to defending our three precious deities, our water, our trees, our earth. And so the men of my generation learnt to stand strong, first against the white man, driving him away with our bows and arrows. And now the brown man who has made something called the nation. That is the story I want to tell you.

PEON. You mean there's more?

GREAT-GRANDPA. What do you mean more? That is the real story. I have seen your school history books. They were big books. When I asked you what they said about us, you said 'Nothing'. Nothing about people who have lived in this land for thousands of years. And now you measure their story by the running hands of that thing on your wrist. Why are you so impatient? You have lost the patience of our tribe.

The summer comes when it comes, and so too the rains. Do you say to them: why don't you come earlier and go sooner? Birds lay eggs. Do mother birds say to their eggs: hatch fast? We sow seeds. Can we say to the grain: grow now?

PEON. Sorry, Great-grandpa. I get it. Now tell me your story

GREAT-GRANDPA (*flares up but in a controlled way*). My story? My story? It's our story. It's your story.

PEON. Sorry, Great-grandpa. Tell me our story. Tell me my story.

GREAT-GRANDPA. I was a young man when it happened. Some men and women came from the city carrying flags with the green of our trees, the orange of our fruits, the white of our doves and the deep blue of our river. They shouted and sang and told us we were free. We said: it is good that you are free. They said: not only we. All of us are free, the people of the jungles and fields, of cities and villages. We are a nation now. A free nation. When they had gone, we laughed long and loud. Had we not always been free? Those of us who had gone to school and college told us this was a different freedom. It was a freedom of the brown man from the white man. This nation now belongs to brown men, they said. Have the brown men killed the white men, we asked. No, they said. They have driven them away, back to where they belong. With bows and arrows, we asked. No. Without bows and arrows, they said. With satyagraha that someone called Gandhi taught them.

PEON. They were talking about Mahatma Gandhi and the Quit India movement.

GREAT-GRANDPA. Don't bring your knowledge into this.

PEON. Sorry, Great-grandpa.

GREAT-GRANDPA. After this freedom, some of us forest dwellers were invited to a place called Delhi. We told the new rulers that we wanted to preserve our homes and live in peace. The new rulers were very polite. They said: let us discuss the problem. There was no problem as far as we could see. But the five men went, one from each forest, with Ram Dayal Munda as their leader.



PEON. You mean Birsa Munda.

GREAT-GRANDPA. I told you to keep your knowledge to yourself. Birsa Munda lived long ago and died long ago. I have heard about him and I shall tell you his story.

PEON. Now, Great-grandpa? I mean won't you first finish your . . . our . . . my story?

GREAT-GRANDPA. I will I will. Don't be impatient.

PEON. Sorry, Great-grandpa.

GREAT-GRANDPA. So the five men went to Delhi and were driving to the house of a man called Nehru . . .

PEON. That's Jawahar . . . sorry, Great-grandpa.

GREAT-GRANDPA. . . . when the police stopped them.

PEON. Why?

GREAT-GRANDPA. Because they couldn't go to this big man's house by horse, they said.

PEON. By horse? You mean they were riding horses?

GREAT-GRANDPA. No. The horses were pulling a cart in which they were sitting.

PEON. That would be a horse . . . sorry.

GREAT-GRANDPA. You interrupt too much.

PEON. Sorry, sorry. I want to hear about the police.

GREAT-GRANDPA. Ram Dayal Munda said to the police: Mr Nehru expects us. If you won't let us pass, we will go back and you can tell him why. The police got scared. We know them, don't we? They will beat and kill till you show them your teeth. Then they'll tuck in their tails and run. (*A very small and bitter chuckle. Peon, relieved, laughs loud and long*) Are you here to listen to your story or to laugh like a hyena?

PEON. To listen to my story.

GREAT-GRANDPA. So listen, then. When our men returned from the visit, they were shaking their heads. They held a meeting and got up one by one to tell us what had happened. This is what they said. 'They didn't understand what we were saying to them. They spoke instead of things like independence, unity, development. Independence from whom? Unity with whom? Development for whom? They explained. There would be roads and water and health and education. We said health and education are good. But roads? We have our paths. Water? We have our river. Our God has given us everything we need . . . the forest, the river, the land. We live off them and we are happy. We want nothing more. We told them that there was a time when we became greedy and our God hid from us. We couldn't see him. The men in Delhi didn't understand us. They didn't understand that if we were left alone to live our lives, we would be happy and they would be happy. They could then be as independent and united as they wanted. But they had no ears that would enable them to hear what we were saying. They thought we were fighting against their nation. They didn't understand what we meant by freedom. We didn't understand what they meant by nation. The five men sat with us looking defeated. I think that good man Baba was talking about this when he said, 'There was a moment in history when . . .

PEON (*completes the sentence which he has heard repeated many times*) . . . when another kind of nation could have been imagined into being where the tribals would have lived their lives in peace and harmony and their forests would have been safe from harm. But the gods of the new rulers were different from our gods. They did not grow angry and hide when people grew greedy.'

GREAT-GRANDPA. I did not know what he meant. But I can't forget his voice. It was full of sadness, like the weeping bird.

PEON. Why do you always talk about the weeping bird? Nobody else in this village has ever heard him.

GREAT-GRANDPA. The weeping bird is sadness. I hear the weeping bird sigh, sob and fall silent. Then sigh, sob and fall silent. It mourns some loss we don't know of. I always thought Baba mourned a dream that had died like a seed that never grew into a tree. I listened to our men who went to Delhi and what I understood is this: the men in Delhi didn't understand that the mango tree is not the tendu tree, though both are trees. People are like that. Some live by the sea, some in the hills, some around rivers and some in the forests. The men who went by horse to meet the new rulers, they said: we are happy in the forest. We are like you, but we will not be happy outside the forest. We have been free because of the forest. Let us be what we are.

But that was not to be. Our men were not able to negotiate peace and harmony for us. We will have to fight for what we have always had . . . our water, trees and earth. We fought for them against the white man. We have been fighting for them against the brown man. May the Sun God give us strength.

*Long silence.*

There it goes.

PEON. What?

GREAT-GRANDPA. The weeping bird. Do you not hear it? There it is. A sigh, a sob and silence. A sigh, a sob and silence. It is growing dark. The weeping bird will sleep. But when it wakes, it will weep again. You are silent, my son. Our story has ended. I hope you will remember it, and when the time comes, remember also those five men who went to Delhi and what they said. We cannot have the peace we want. So we must fight for it. How strange. To fight for peace. But there's no other way. We don't want to anger our gods again.

*Blackout.*

## ACT 2

### Scene 1

*Peon enters front stage in a T-shirt and jeans, looking back. Ma's voice is heard, singing 'Maili chadar'. The song fades.*

PEON (*momentarily overcome. Shakes himself out of it*). I wouldn't say I'm soft. No. Can't afford to be soft. But that song . . . that song rings in my head. I've heard Ma sing it only once. But it has stayed in here (*touches his heart*). I never know when it is going to start. But when it does, it makes my eyes prick. The words, the sentiment, the tune . . . 'How can I come to you my lord / Wearing this much-stained shawl? / You sent me to this world / In a skin that was clean and pure / But living this worldly life, / I stained it more and more / How do I clean myself now / Of a lifetime's shameful stains / How can I come to you my lord / Wearing this much-stained shawl?'

It stirs your conscience, doesn't it?

But let's get on with the story. Jeet was lost to my bosses, to his mother, to Karan, to Sharmishtha. Not for one year or two. But a whole 12 years. A tapa. He went away a young man of 22. He came back a mature man of 34. Meanwhile, everybody had grown that much older.

*Steps out of one wing. TOP office lights up. Thadani, Oak and Patel are at their desk. Peon enters through the other wing, dressed in his office clothes.*

OAK. I was thinking of introducing the poetry round this year again.

PATEL. Once bitten never shy.

OAK. I was shy for 11 years after the Jeet fiasco.

PATEL. Keep it that way. What do you get out of poetry? Fancy falsehoods.

THADANI. I think we need to introduce something cultural. We're supposed to be a cultural body. Our leadership selections should be like college festivals for them to catch on. Young people are sentimental. They all write poetry. Everybody can't paint. Everybody can't sing. But everybody can rhyme one word with another.

PATEL. Why not dance? You should see these reality shows. Oak, do you watch television?

OAK. I watch the BBC.

PATEL. And he talks of patriotism.

OAK. Having a broad viewpoint doesn't prevent me from being patriotic.

PATEL. But you should watch reality shows. That will rid your mind of fusty ideas about young people. They aren't what they were in our times. Or even Jeet's. Let's have dance.

THADANI. But dance is plain entertainment. No thought. Leadership is all about conveying thoughts through words. Words carry meaning, feeling, belief. Dance doesn't.

PATEL. Dance tells young people we are not fuddy-duddies. It makes them apply for our programme. Last year, we had only three applicants. The bosses are asking us to close down our branch. This is the time to show we can get in the numbers. Otherwise, we'll have to pack up and go home.

THADANI. You have a point. What do you think Oak? If Jeet had returned and started showing the world what our programme does for young people, we'd have been on firm ground. But as things stand . . . (*Peon goes out and returns with a note which he puts on the table. Thadani picks it up and reads*) 'Shri Jeetendra-ji would like to see you at your convenience.'

OAK. Shri Jeetendra-ji? Were you expecting someone, Patel? Thadani?

PEON. I think it is Jeet.

THADANI. Our Jeet?

OAK. How do you know?

PEON. I know the man who brought it. He's from our village. He said, 'A note from Jeet.'

PATEL. He said that? A man from your village said Jeet?

PEON. It's not like that. In the village, people always called him Jeet. He used to come with Baba during the school holidays to play with the children.

THADANI. OK, OK. (*Scribbles a note and gives it to Peon*) Give this to the man. (*Peon leaves.*)

OAK. What did you write?

THADANI. 'Dear Shri Jeetendra-ji, your convenience is our convenience. Come whenever it suits you.'

PATEL. I object. Why should we sound humble?

THADANI. Ironic, Patel. Ironic. (*Claps. Peon steps forward.*) Get some good biscuits. And brew the tea well. Lots of milk. Lots of sugar. It's not money from your pocket.

PATEL. He never stints on milk and sugar. I've noticed there's always more tea in the pot than we need. That's his cut.

OAK. That's OK, Patel. That's OK. (*Jeet stands at a distance and clears his throat. They look up. Jeet folds his hands humbly but doesn't step forward.*) Arrewah, Jeet. I wouldn't have recognized you if . . . But come in, come in.

THADANI (*pointedly*). Not Jeet, Oak. Jeetendra-ji. Is that right?

JEET (*unabashed*). As it happens, yes. I was renamed at the end of the course.

PATEL. Why? Prince wasn't.

JEET. You're right. He wasn't. They thought his name suited him very well. They thought for the work I was destined to do, I should have a more substantial name than Jeet.

THADANI. They?

JEET. The pramukh and upa-pramukh of the Pathfinders. They gave us our certificates at the end of the course and interviewed some of us afterwards.

OAK. That's interesting. It's the first time they've done that.

JEET. Perhaps they didn't feel too certain of the leadership qualities of the earlier participants. The man who is ruling us now is proof.

PATEL. They think your leadership qualities surpass his? He's a very senior man and soaked in experience.

JEET. I don't know. They said so. They said the state was falling apart. That's why they sent me for the advanced course.

PATEL. Advanced course? What's that? They didn't send Prince.

JEET (*looking embarrassed for the first time*). No. They thought he was naturally sharp.

PATEL (*laughs, pleased*). That he is. That he is.

*Peon comes in with tea and biscuits. Pours out four cups and places them before the four men. Jeet looks at him and smiles. He smiles back.*

JEET (*to Peon, pushing away his cup*). I've had my tea. You know I have only one cup in the afternoon.

*Silence while the others sip their tea.*

OAK. You could have told us about this development, don't you think?

JEET. Which?

OAK. The advanced course. And how long it would last.

JEET. I wanted to write to you. But they said they would. Didn't they?

*The three men exchange glances.*

THADANI. They probably forgot. But where was this advanced course?

JEET. I am not allowed to say. I can only say it was further into the mountains in an ashram. I was to get instruction in many things from the chief swami and read all the books on a list I was given.

OAK. Kautilya's *Arthashastra*?

JEET (*laughs heartily*). When you sent me, I wasn't allowed to tell even my mother where I was going. Now you . . .

THADANI. You mean they have sworn you to secrecy even about the books you read?

JEET. Yes, well . . .

OAK. (*swiftly changing the subject*). So how is she?

JEET. Who?

OAK. Your mother?

JEET (*with a closed face*). Older. (*Pause. Softening*) Unhappier.

OAK. Ah, yes. And your friends? Karan? Sharmishtha?

JEET. I'll meet them this evening. I'm sure they're fine.

*Peon clears away the tea things.*

JEET. May I go now? This was just a preliminary courtesy call.

THADANI. So what's your plan now?

JEET. Whatever they say. I think they're planning a lecture tour of the state for me.

OAK. I see. Towards what end?

JEET. Next year's Assembly elections. So that people get to know me. Unknowns don't get elected.

THADANI. You've made up your mind to jump into politics.

JEET. Oh, yes. That's my destiny. They said so and I know it now. The more I read and thought, the more convinced I became that they were right. I needed these years away from . . . from . . . all this to declutter my mind. To understand myself. That's what tapascharya is all about isn't it? Self-knowledge. It took me 12 years, a full tapa, to achieve it.

*The three men are bemused. They nod slowly.*

JEET (*stands up and humbly folds his* hands). Before I leave, I have a request to make. I would like to employ this man (*indicating Peon*). I came to trust him completely when he was with me. I will need men around me now whom I can trust.

THADANI. I am sorry, Jeetendra-ji. We trust him too. I hope you don't mind if we don't grant your request.

JEET. Not at all. I didn't expect you would. (*Stands for a moment looking them all in the eye. Then folds his hands again and walks out.*)

THADANI. There goes our man. We cannot hold out like this, you know. We really must break away from the Pathfinders. Our visions are different. We are looking to create strong men who . . .

OAK. And women

THADANI. Sorry?

OAK. Strong men and women who . . .

THADANI. Yes, of course . . . who may or may not enter politics but will share our vision in whatever they do. While they want men who will win elections. Machine men with brains to know which way to steer the machine.

*Patel claps. Peon steps forward.*

PATEL. You sent us a report every day while you were with him. But there must have been many things you didn't report.

PEON. Sir, I reported everything according to the columns on the proforma.

PATEL. Sure. But the proforma didn't ask about everything, did it?

PEON. There was very little time to do anything else.

PATEL. So why does he say he came to trust you?

PEON. It surprised me when he said that. I only did what I was asked to do. By you.

OAK. But that's it, isn't it? That's the kind of man one trusts. The man who does everything he is told to do.

THADANI. And no questions asked.

PATEL. Are you happy here?

PEON. Happy? (*Laughs apologetically*) I get two meals. I have a place to sleep. I have a wife and three children in the village. I must be happy.

OAK. Thank you . . . what's your name by the way?

PEON. It's OK, sir. You don't need it. Just clap and I will come. As always.

*Oak nods thoughtfully. Peon walks away with the tea tray.*

## Scene 2

*Ma is sitting up on her cot. Jeet paces up and down like a caged tiger in the small space available in her room.*

JEET. Don't weaken me with the words of a man who is deeply obliged to you for taking him in when his parents died. He will always agree with you. He loves losing his way in a maze of ifs and buts . . . words that block action. I am not like that. I want everything to be clear cut. There is right and there is wrong. Every situation in life or politics presents you with multiple alternatives. You must know which to choose. As I will need to between people and people. You and Karan and Sharmishtha have chosen your people. I will choose mine. The world is too vast for one human heart to embrace. It splits in the attempt. I want my heart to be whole and strong. I have made my choice, Ma. My father's was another age. The age of idealism. We have moved on. We are pragmatists. We do what is best in the given circumstances. If we have the guts, we MAKE the circumstances that will support what we want to do. We aim high. We aspire. I want to toss a coin and come up winners, whether it's heads or tails. It will hurt you if I say so, but in today's terms, your husband my father, was a loser.

MA (*long pause as she studies Jeet's face*). It is not that your heart is too small to embrace the world, son. But you have allowed it to grow too hard.

JEET. That is a sign of dedication to my cause, Ma. Think of a sitarist. He practises day and night. As a result, he has hard, calloused fingertips. For 12 years, I have hammered my heart into shape so that I may shape the future of our country. I have practised ways of reaching into people's hearts. I have addressed mountain people to see if, despite their ignorance of my language, they are moved by what I say. I have exercised my body cruelly, so that it will not fail me when I travel the length and breadth of this land, lighting the fire of patriotism in every heart. If in the process my heart has hardened, it is only in the eyes of the bleeding hearts of the world. To every other man, woman and child, a hard heart and dry eyes are signs of strength. He is a lion of a man, they say, and put their trust in him.

MA. You have developed a persuasive tongue, my son. Yes. A hard heart has its advantages in the field you have chosen. But this is what I have to say against a hard heart: it stifles the conscience and ultimately kills it. Perhaps that is what you want in the service of your vision. So, what is this vision? What do you see before you? Your eyes are restless. They do not meet mine as they did before you went away. What do they see?

JEET. The future, Ma, the future. I see it shine under a radiant sun. I see gleaming roads, splendid buildings, enterprise, wealth. I see men, women and children go about their work with smiles on their faces.

MA. I did not ask for a cascade of words, Jeet. I asked for brass tacks. Men, women and children is a meaningless phrase. Men are both those who have four meals a day and those who have none. Where do the starving millions stand in your vision?

JEET. Nowhere. because, in my vision there will be no starving millions.

MA. Because they are dead of hunger and disease?

JEET. Oh, Ma! You joke. Because I will carry that part of my father's vision into the future. They shall have food. They shall have clothes. They shall have shelter.

MA. Will our Adivasis have rights to their land?

JEET. Why not? And even when they don't, they will benefit from the use we will put the land to.

MA. That fills me with foreboding. To me it says the old story continues. (*Long pause.*) And Sharmishtha? Will she agree to all this? She has become even more deeply involved with the clinic since I took ill.

JEET (*stops his restless pacing and sits down beside Ma. Takes her hand in his*). I am sorry I wasn't here to take care of you. But Karan did, didn't he?

MA. He did. Yes. So did Sharmishtha. They took turns day and night to make sure I had all I needed. As long as they are with you, I will not worry.

JEET (*his tone is tender*). Don't worry, Ma, whether they are with me or not. I have chosen a different path, but I am still yours and Baba's son. You must trust me. (*He sits down by her feet.*) You think my heart is hard. It is not, Ma. It is not hard at all. Many are the times I have wept in the mountains thinking of you, Sharmishtha, Karan, knowing full well I was walking into a world very far from yours. I took great pains to harden my heart because in this new world, I could not afford to be vulnerable. I needed to at least pretend I was not. But inside this shell there is a softness for those who mean the world to me. Please say you trust me, Ma. I don't know when I will have the time to see you again like this. I need your trust. And your blessings. Please bless me, Ma.

MA. May I tell you a little story before that? This was when you were a boy.

JEET (*laughing*), Not that one, please.

MA. I have never told you this one.

JEET. I can't believe it. You've told me every single story about when I was a boy. I suspect some of them were made up for the moral at the end.

MA (*laughing*), Perhaps I made up a few. But this one is not made up. And I have only just remembered it because the occasion calls for it.

JEET. Is it long? I have to go.

MA. I will make it as brief as I can. Once we had gone to your grandfather's place. There was an open space there where he had put in a swing and a see-saw. You and your cousin played on them all day. But then you came home crying. Because each time the seesaw came down on your side, your cousin laughed at you from his height.

JEET. So children cry.

MA. You hated coming down. And you hated being laughed at.

JEET. But isn't that natural?

MA. Perhaps it is. Perhaps I worry unnecessarily. Like mothers everywhere. How will he deal with the world, I wondered? How will the world deal with him? Pure, irrational worry.

JEET (*hugging her. Gently*). Don't worry, Ma. Trust me. And bless me.

*Ma blesses him. He rises and walks slowly but firmly away. Ma looks after him for a long time, tears streaming down her cheeks.*

*Blackout.*

## Scene 3

*The same bench as in Scene 4. Sharmishtha in deep thought. She looks at her watch. Looks into the wing. Takes out her cell phone from her handbag and is about to press the buttons when Jeet hurries in.*

JEET. Hi. Sorry. I got held up.

SHARMISHTHA. And who are you?

JEET (*laughs*). Come on.

SHARMISHTHA. No, I mean it. Twelve years of not knowing where a man is, is like twelve years of not knowing a man. It's bizarre. I don't think this has happened to any woman before. Except Damayanti.

JEET. Or Penelope.

SHARMISHTHA. Who's that?

JEET. Never mind. She's from another culture.

SHARMISHTHA. Had I been living in Mahabharata times, I would have sent emissaries to the mountains to ask every man they met 'How much of a man is a person who not only deserts his fiancée but leaves no address?'

JEET. If your emissary had tracked me down, I would have answered, 'Not much of a man at all. Sounds like a scoundrel to me. Tell the fiancée to forget him and marry someone else.' Like that song of Mukesh's. (*Sings the refrain of* '*Aansoo bhari hai*') Which film is that from?

SHARMISHTHA. I don't know and I don't want to know. But are you trying to tell me something, Jeet?

JEET (*laughs*). You know what they've named me now?

SHARMISHTHA. Who is they?

JEET. The Pathfinders who are guiding my life.

SHARMISHTHA. Why? You lost your own will in the mountains?

JEET. Sharmu, Sharmu, Sharmu. Twelve years, but your tongue hasn't lost its edge.

SHARMISHTHA. Some things remain constant, Jeet . . . sorry, you were telling me about your new name that THEY have given you.

JEET. No need to be sarcastic. They are an extremely well-organized and idealistic group of responsible and thinking individuals who have our country's best interests at heart.

SHARMISHTHA. And they see you as their agent?

JEET. They see me as my own man, Sharmu. You have to believe that. I am what I am. They said I was a raw diamond that only needed cutting and polishing.

SHARMISHTHA. They sound like a bunch of Suratis.

JEET. Your Gujarati roots show even after two generations of your people living here.

SHARMISHTHA. I hope your forest roots have remained as strong as mine these twelve years. Or have they frozen and died in the cold?

JEET. Sharmishtha, I think we need to be serious.

SHARMISHTHA. I am serious. My last question troubles me. Your new name whatever it is troubles me. The song you sang troubles me. I am only pretending to be light-hearted. Inside me, my heart is a tight ball, Jeet. I am afraid. (*Long silence. Jeet gets up and starts walking around. He turns and is about to speak.*) No, Jeet. If you are going to say something about our future, you must sit beside me, look me in the eyes and speak.

*Jeet remains standing for a long time looking at her, then straightens his shoulders and sits down beside her.*

JEET. They have named me Jeetendra Sinh. They wanted me to have a strong name. Name, manner, voice, everything matters when you are out to win people's minds and hearts. Only then can you win them over to your ideas.

SHARMISHTHA. And what are those ideas?

JEET. Briefly put, we believe in discipline, development and patriotism. We believe our people are not mature enough to use their rights for the national good. They need a higher authority to hold their hands, push them on occasion, even rap them on the knuckles. We believe in doing this firmly but with love. The majority of our people don't think. They are led by emotion. That can be bad. But it can also be good. We can work with emotions to achieve our goals. That is why our target is the young. They have a natural energy and passion. And they are open. They take easily to new ideas. He who owns the youth, gains the future. That is why TOP organizes these leadership festivals for the young.

SHARMISHTHA. TOP are connected to these Pathfinders?

JEET. Of course. They look after the cultural affairs of the organization in this region.

*Long silence. Jeet stands uncertainly, looking at her, then looks away.*

SHARMISHTHA. And now you have something to tell me. I can see it in your eyes, your gestures, everything. Maybe I can help you. You are calling off our relationship.

JEET (*confused by her directness*). Only because I don't think you would want to be part of my life now.

SHARMISHTHA. You're dead right I won't. You're a different Jeet from the one I knew. (*Pause*) And loved.

JEET. I am sorry. I am really deeply sorry.

SHARMISHTHA. Don't be sorry. I was prepared for it. But the saddest thing is, I look at you now and feel . . . nothing. It was a beautiful thing . . . our love.

JEET (*very hurt*). Don't say that, Sharmu. I am still deeply fond of you. I would still marry you if you didn't have such strong ideas about right and wrong and . . .

SHARMISHTHA. Yes, yes, yes. That is a huge drawback. It won't work. Anyway, marriage never meant anything to me. I was looking forward to a life of shared ideas and ideals. That dream is dead. But I will keep it alive. Alone. (*Stands up*) Perhaps it's time to say goodbye.

JEET (*stands up*). Wait a bit, Sharmu. Karan is coming. We'll sit and chat. Like old times.

SHARMISHTHA (*shakes her head*). The old times are over. You know it. I know it. We have never pretended earlier. Why pretend now? (*Holds out her hand. He spreads his arms for a hug. She does not respond. He takes her hand, holds it, then lets it go. She walks away.*)

JEET. Sharmishtha, I still love you. (*She keeps walking.*) You are a good woman. (*She is gone. He stands looking lost. Then squares his shoulders.*) We must do a little wrong to do a great right. I grant I have wronged you, Sharmu. But one day you'll thank me for it. Together, we would have destroyed each other. Apart, we will live and thrive while still sharing the burden of making the world a better place to live in. You in your way. I in mine.

*Blackout.*

**Scene 4**

*The TOP office. Thadani, Oak and Patel in their usual places, Peon in his.*

PATEL. So we are to be reduced to a back-up operation.

OAK. We were always that, Patel.

PATEL. But not quite so obviously.

THADANI. We deluded ourselves into thinking we were autonomous. That's our fault.

PATEL. We were given to understand that we were.

OAK. Only insofar as organizing youth festivals went. After all, we are on the Pathfinders' payroll.

PATEL. Payroll is a big word for what they give us. Surely, we aren't here for that? Thadani, are you here for that? You must be making piles as a cardiologist. Even a part-time one.

THADANI (*smiles*). There are piles and there are piles. I dare not talk about mine in your presence, Patel.

OAK. Look. Let's get things into perspective. We were Pathfinder men from our schooldays, right? We could have opted out any time. We weren't shackled. But we didn't. Why? Because their vision became our vision. We stayed in the fold through our working lives. Then we thought just making money and existing didn't make sense. We had to pay back to society. And what better way than to take forward the ideas we had grown up with? We've been autonomous in our professions. (*Glancing at Thadani and Patel*) Yes, even I, as head of department, Botany. Nobody could tell me how to teach, how to fire those young minds with my passion for the subject.

PATEL. And now, a young twerp we pulled off his college bench will lord it over us.

THADANI. Sorry. That's not how it is. Our orders will come from above. So will his. We will be autonomous in our work, the twerp as you call him will be autonomous in his.

PATEL. Does he have it in him to be that? I cannot forget the poetry. And the genes he has inherited.

THADANI. You suffer from a whopping gene obsession, man.

OAK. Listen, Patel. Culture is an evolutionary force. Why do you think those wily men in the mountains kept Jeet away from his environment for a whole tapa? It was to graft upon his native genes a stronger, more sophisticated culture. His native genes had produced a thinking, sensitive man who read deeply, spoke well and wrote with style. We need men like that. The Pathfinders were wise enough to see that. But his reading needed to be guided, his ideas channelled, his speech given polish. The aim was to produce a hardy hybrid, more colourful, more attractive than the original. Its nurture is now in their hands. Only they know what manure this new plant needs, to make it thrive and grow in the right direction.

PATEL. Wow! Now we know how you held your classes captive!

*They all laugh.*

PEON. Jeetendra-ji is here.

*The TOP trio straighten up, assume serious looks and nod. Peon leads Jeet in.*

JEET. Namaste. (*Folds his hands formally, but humbly.*)

*The three men return the greeting somewhat awkwardly.*

OAK. Please take a seat Jeet . . err . . . endra-ji.

JEET (*laughs with genuine amusement as he lowers himself into the chair*). That name's going to trip you up for a while. Why don't you stick to Jeet? Only between us, of course. Publicly, it'll have to be the other. So, what's the plan?

THADANI (*pulling out a map*). This is your constituency. Mostly middle-class Hindu. But there is this huge spread on the side moving into the hills. That's the forests and the Vanvasis. They have never trusted the old man. But they will have an instinctive trust in you.

JEET. I don't like that word.

THADANI. Which?

JEET. Vanvasis. It merely describes them by their native terrain. We must call them by their proper name. Adivasis. Adi, the first, vasi, inhabitant. The first inhabitants of this land. (*TOP trio exchange glances.*) You look confused. Don't. You show your respect when you call people by their proper names. That's how they trust you.

PATEL. Good strategy.

JEET (*eyes hooded*). I don't think you should call it that, Mr Patel. Truth cannot be described as a strategy.

PATEL. Ah yes, of course.

JEET. So, what's the plan?

OAK. We have arranged for a four-stop tour. The old warhorse will accompany you.

JEET. Really? That's not going to be comfortable for him.

OAK. We'll make it comfortable. As five time-MLA, he will always speak first. Then you come on.

JEET. Pre-publicity? People don't know me.

THADANI. That will be arranged.

OAK. We are already working on your speeches.

JEET (*stands up. Paces. Stops*). That's not what I was given to understand.

THADANI. What?

JEET. That I will make readymade speeches.

THADANI. Well . . . that's always been the way.

OAK. Please, sit down. You seem agitated. We are only discussing . . .

JEET. That was not discussing. That was telling.

THADANI. Sorry. But won't you sit down?

JEET. I think better on my feet. (*After a few more moments of pacing*) Look, the speeches I write come from the heart. A prepared speech comes from the tongue. Our aim is to capture hearts and minds. That can't be done by mouthing words. It is done with heartfelt words. Those words will have to be mine.

*A long silence. The three men are giving themselves time to think. Jeet stands before them, looking straight down at them. It is suggestive of their new power equation. TOP's body language changes.*

OAK. Yes, of course. And with your wonderful flair which all of us were witness to . . . weren't we . . . your examples from world literature, your references to our myths . . . you should . . . you should of course write your own speeches. Will you have tea? (*He claps. The tension dissolves.*)

THADANI. So, returning to the tour. (*Referring to the map*) After addressing our businessmen here and our Muslim brethren there, you will move to the Dalit colonies and finally the . . .

JEET. Adivasi villages.

*Peon comes in with a tea tray.*

JEET. Logistics?

PATEL. Prince is in charge of that.

JEET. Oh? So that's decided?

PATEL. Yes. He is to be your right-hand man.

JEET (*nods thoughtfully*). That's good. Very, very good. He's sharp.

PATEL. That he is.

JEET. And not troubled by that thing called conscience which I can't always repress and which gets in the way of our grander plans.

*Awkward silence.*

PATEL. Well . . . conscience . . . he does . . . I mean of course he has a conscience. He's been brought up right. With all the values of our culture.

JEET. I meant no offence, Mr Patel. I was being complimentary.

THADANI. Come on, Patel. You should take it as a compliment.

JEET (*getting up*). I must go. I am meeting a friend.

PATEL. Karan?

JEET. As a matter of fact, yes. (*Near the wings. Glances at Peon.*) And by the way. I'll be needing this man.

*The three men look surprised. They open their mouths to protest, then close them. Silence while they gather their wits.*

OAK. Yes, of course, if you think he'll be of help.

JEET. He'll be of great help. We spent a whole year together. He knows my habits. And I found him to be very discreet.

THADANI. Oh? (*The three men give Peon suspicious looks*) Oh, yes. Sure. He is that. Very discreet. He wouldn't have lasted in this office otherwise. (*Looking at Peon*) Would you like to go?

PEON (*gaze lowered to the floor*). Whatever the bosses say, sir.

*Jeet nods and goes off. The three men glower after him, then look reproachfully at Peon. But he is still staring at the floor.*

*Blackout.*

## Scene 5

*Peon enters laughing, wearing his colourful shirt.*

I'm hitching my wagon to a rising star
I'm hitching my wagon to a rising star
The mountain men are wily and wise
With money enough to make us rise
So here's my chance, here's my chance
So here's my chance to sing and dance!

Got to set up a couple of tree stumps for Jeet and Karan. Things are cooking up nice and spicy, with all sorts of people stirring the pot. I just have to keep my eyes and ears open, and life will provide all the fun I want. (*Goes out dancing and returns in his neutral shirt-pant, carrying a couple of wooden blocks.*)

*Jeet and Karan enter, talking.*

JEET. You're not going to put emotional fences in my way, Karan. I know Ma is worried. It is perhaps in the nature of mothers to worry. And it is in the nature of sons to break away, make their choices and win back their mothers' trust. I intend to do just that. You will see. Meanwhile, I need you to be with me.

*They sit down on the tree stumps.*

KARAN. These used to be trees. I remember them well. Massive. Offering their shade to us when we sat here in the heat of the sun after college.

JEET. Yes. I remember them too. But not sentimentally. What was, was. What is, is. What will be is in our hands.

KARAN. Thinking of trees that once were is not sentimentality. It is looking at history to figure out our way ahead which, as you say, is in our hands. Are we OK with these being stumps? Or should they still have been trees? Those are the questions we need to ask and answer.

JEET. You have already answered them for yourself, Karan. For you, they should have been trees. But then we'd have had fewer books. I have come to face the fact that human progress is brutal. We've been cutting down trees forever. There's only one way to go ahead. Ensure that some good comes of the trees we cut down.

KARAN. That begs another question: Good for whom?

JEET (*impatient*). For the nation, of course. And so for its people.

KARAN. People in general, or people in particular?

JEET. Am I in the dock, by any chance?

KARAN. You will be, Jeet, once you're a full-fledged politician. People of every stripe and colour will ask you questions. There will also be those who don't have a voice to ask you questions. Their questions will simmer within them till one day they will spit fire.

JEET. You should write plays, not poetry.

*Both laugh.*

JEET. But I'm not side-stepping your question. You are referring to our Adivasis. You think these wonderful, peace-loving people are capable of spitting fire?

KARAN. They did once, against the British.

JEET. That was a foreign power. We are not. We will develop them. They live only for today, with no thought for the future. We will show them a radiant future, one in which they will be equal beneficiaries of the wealth created by our entrepreneurs and industrialists.

KARAN. Using *their* natural wealth and livelihoods. In short, you see them as the brown man's burden.

JEET. You are being utterly unfair. Isn't it because the Adivasis are our people that we want to bring them out of ignorance into the light of civilization?

KARAN. But that is exactly what the British thought they were doing to us. That imperialism was motivated by a high-minded desire to uplift people of colour. In their frankest moments, they called us barbarians.

JEET (*huffily*). We don't call Adivasis that.

KARAN. But we have always treated them that way.

*Long silence. The two friends look at each other without blinking.*

JEET. Sometimes, words are no more than air. Actions speak. My actions will show you what I believe. (*Pause*) I have a long way to walk before I can get to where I want to be. Here and now, my power to act is limited. Look, Karan. We have been together through our youth. You have been my adopted brother. I want you to be with me through this journey too. (*Karan is about to speak*) No. Not actively. But as a sounding board. Even adversary. Over the next two years, I will be in the inescapable company of Prince. I am asking you for succour. You must attend each of the four meetings I am scheduled to address—

KARAN. Don't tell me!

JEET. What?

KARAN. Prince, of all people? He recited Browning's superb poem as though it were a dictionary of the world's most difficult words.

JEET. 'Let me have men about me that are fat, / Sleek-headed men and such as sleep a-nights.'

KARAN. And then Caesar was stabbed in the back by all the fat, sleek-headed senators of Rome

JEET. You're incorrigible. Show you the waxing moon, and you'll say it will soon wane.

KARAN. Laws of Nature. No man has escaped them. So, what were you saying about these meetings?

JEET. I'm going to be on the road. I'm to be given a position in the PPP . . .

KARAN. You've officially joined the Pathfinder People's Party?

JEET. Yes. To justify my appearance on stage with old man Thakur. Prince has also been given an official position. I am to address four meetings in my constituency. Thakur speaks first, then I. All four meetings are happening during the college vacations. So there's no excuse for you not to be there. I'll get TOP to arrange a car to bring you to the venues directly.

KARAN. Jeet, you know I . . .

JEET. I'm not taking no for an answer. I need you to be there, Karan. Look, we may have different ideas about the future of this country, but friendship should go beyond such differences. Shouldn't it?

KARAN (*looks at him warily, then softens and smiles*). It should.

JEET. And it will?

KARAN. It will.

JEET (*stands up.*) There's hard work ahead. Speeches to write and practise.

KARAN. Practise?

JEET. Hitler did too. Assiduously. Don't look shocked. We must separate his ideas from his methods. He stood before a mirror and practised to get his gestures just right. Paid painstaking attention to his image. Worked on every detail of his speeches—the words, the throw of the voice, the pauses, everything. Once he'd mastered all this, then he was free to pay attention to the camera. It was important for his image that he stayed in people's minds through his photographs, long after the fiery speeches were over. If you want to hold the people in the palm of your hand, to fire them up with your ideas, you need to do rigorous homework. (*He is suddenly in his own world.*)

KARAN. But Hitler, Jeet?

JEET. Why not? I just told you. One need not share his ideology. But one can use his techniques.

KARAN. His technique was to lie through his teeth.

JEET. No. His technique was to convince people he was speaking the truth while he was lying through his teeth.

KARAN. Why should you need such a technique, if your purpose isn't to lie?

JEET. Karan, Karan, Karan, we are not in a college debate. I realized during my training why you always won those. Not because your ideas were better. That really doesn't count. But your voice was stronger. I have worked hard on mine. When your voice is stronger, you sound more confident. When you sound confident, people believe you are smarter than you perhaps are. We are in realpolitik, Karan. This is war, and I am going to win it. Just come and hear me. Then tell me whether you heard falsehood as falsehood. That's the power of oratory. (*Karan looks bemused.*) That was a stupid thing to say. Of course, you'll hear falsehood as falsehood. But you might be the only one in the gathering who will. Anyway, I'm not going to go around uttering falsehoods just for the heck of it. They might fool the people. But not the media. That should assure you. I must rush now. See you at my first meeting. Shantinagar. (*He hurries out.*)

*Karan sits looking at the ground as the light fades.*

## Scene 6

*The stage is bare except for a single chair. Peon hurries in with a mirror on wheels. Sets it up carefully. Throughout his chatter, he is busy polishing it, using various fluids and waxes. By the end, we are to assume there is not a speck of dust on it.*

PEON. Today is the last meeting. He will address my people. They are very eager to hear him. They saw him as a boy. Now they will see him as a grown man. An important man. Makes a difference, no? When I was a boy, I wore either a shirt or half pants. Never both together. When I wore the shirt, my pants were hanging up to dry. When I wore my pants, my shirt was hanging up to dry. The shirt was long enough to hide my important possessions. The pants kept slipping. I would use the tough tendrils of the banyan to hold them up. Look at me now (*Stops polishing to pose before the mirror.*) This well-cut pair of pants, this fitting shirt—I look like an officer, no? (*Starts polishing again*) Yup. There's a big difference between boy and man. You remember that poem the boss recited which won him the leadership crown? Keep that in your mind when you hear his speech today. What? Of course you'll hear his speech. Why do you think I'm polishing this mirror? He'll dress up, and he'll practise his speech before it.

Mirror mirror on the wall, who's the fairest of them all? The answer has to be: Him. He is fair. Very fair. You've seen that for yourself. As fair as a foreigner. Our people like fair people. They vote for them. That's why they voted for Nehru, right? He was fair. So was his daughter. And the daughter's son. Old man Thakur was also fair. Age has darkened his skin. He must be at least seventy. Much younger than my great-grandfather, but getting on.

There. That's done. (*Looks at his watch*) He'll come any moment now. He's a stickler for time. He says our country has lagged behind the West and Japan and China because we don't care about time. He's going to set all that straight once he comes to power. He's calculated that too. Give me 12 years, he says to me, and you'll see me in the highest chair of this state. Another 12, and I'll be leading the nation. He plans in multiples of 12. (*Looks at his watch again.*) Just one minute and one more job to do. (*Fetches a collection of stoles and drapes them over the back of the chair.*) Now I'll get into position to touch his feet. He likes that. Of course he'll say, 'How many times must I tell you not to do that.' I'll smile humbly and mutter something and . . . Anyway, you'll see all that for yourselves.

*Jeet enters, wearing a crisp white narrow-cut pajama and a cream-coloured kurta. He carries a small roll of paper in his hands. Peon bows to touch his feet.*

JEET (*annoyed*). How many times must I tell you not to do that. If we continue to be feudal, we'll never progress.

PEON (*smiles and mutters*). Sir, I . . .

*Jeet isn't listening. He stands before the mirror. Peon hands him the stoles, one by one. Jeet drapes each one over a shoulder, pulls it across the back and drapes the end over the other arm. Spends a moment studying the effect before moving on to the next. Six stoles later, he holds up three fingers. Peon hands him stole No. 3. Jeet looks at the effect and nods. Stands a little further away. His eyes still on the mirror, he holds out the roll of paper to Peon. Peon steps forward smartly, takes it, steps back and unrolls it.*

JEET. Are you ready? Shall I begin?

PEON. Yes, sir.

JEET (*looking out at an imagined audience of hundreds*). Dear brothers and sisters. I stand before you, a humble member of this great family of which we have been an inseparable part—my father, my mother, my brother Karan, my sister Sharmishtha and I. The elders among you, whose feet I now touch most humbly, have seen me run around naked beneath these trees. Like you, the sky was my cover, the fruit of the trees my food, the water of our crystal stream my life. I have drawn sustenance from this soil. She is my mother. I shall always bow before her and be her true son. Dear brothers and sisters, just as I have shared in your joys, I have shared in your sorrows too. You have never lacked what Nature can give. But you have sorely lacked what man can give. We have seen government after government come and go. Roads and schools have been built, but not for you. Houses and hospitals have been constructed, but not for you. You have not received even a fraction of the benefits that a caring government should and can give. Why? I ask, why? The answer to that question is simple. Because no government so far has thought you worth caring about. Worth caring for. If you got education, it was not from our people. If you got health care, it was not from our people. It was from foreigners who demanded their pound of flesh in return—your souls. Your very souls, my dear brothers and sisters. You were asked to hand over your souls to their God. Many of you did. But we shall repair that damage. We will give you a caring government that will correct all the wrongs done to you. Your children who are now naked will be fully clothed. Your stomachs which are now half-empty will be full. Your roofs which now leak will be made whole. You will inhabit model villages. I say this in the name of my father who gave his life for your welfare. I say this in the name of my mother who even now thinks first of you, then of herself. I say this in the name of my conscience, that most valuable part of ourselves which directs all our actions. I say this in the name of our culture which is best expressed in two words: vasudhaiva kutumbakam. You may not know what that means. But you live the words. And I will live them with you. Vasudhaiva kutumbakam. The world is my family. Our family is not just you and me, yours and ours, it is also all this that we see around us, roots and leaves, feathers and beaks, paws and hide, the worm and the reptile, and, above us all, the immensity of the sky with its moon and sun, its stars and meteors. Vasudhaiva is not just the world—it is the universe. Remember every word I have said to you today. I do not utter empty phrases. My words are the heralds of my actions. I expect you to tally the one with the other. And if they do not match, to raise your voices and tell me so. A great statesman who lived in a country thousands of miles away and hundreds of years ago once said, 'There is no other way to guard yourself against flattery than by making men understand that telling you the truth will not offend you.' I will say so now. Telling me the truth will never offend me. For I live for truth. I hope you will give me the power to work for you. Thank you for listening to me today. Jai Hind!

*Peon, who has been listening mesmerized, breaks into applause.*

JEET (*visibly relaxes. As he approaches the chair to sit, Peon hastily picks up the stoles on its back and stands with them draped over his forearm*). You clapped.

PEON. You were word perfect. I didn't have to prompt you even once. At one point, I stopped looking at the paper. If you had stumbled then, I would have stumbled with you.

JEET. You liked what you heard?

PEON. It was beautiful, sir.

JEET. You think your people will like it?

PEON. I am sure they will, sir.

JEET. You will kindly report their comments to me.

PEON. My people don't say much, sir.

JEET. I know. But if you ask them, they will. You are one of them. (*Pause*) Do you think the outfit is right? I don't want to overdress.

PEON. This is just right, sir. But may I say a churidar would look smarter? And perhaps a Nehru jacket.

JEET. And a rose in the buttonhole? Do you know what you're saying, young man? You are taking us back by half a century. Clothes maketh the man. I know this isn't particularly smart. But better than the flappy pajama and half-sleeved sadra I was made to wear through college. My father's tailor made them for him and me. I had to borrow the jeans and T-shirt I wore for the poetry competition. Simple living and high thinking, they called it. (*Thoughtful pause*) You know something?

PEON. Yes, sir?

JEET. I always longed to have good clothes. (*Looks searchingly at Peon*) You don't look surprised.

PEON. Sir, not making comparison sir between you and me, but I too . . . wanted . . . good clothes. Cotton, silk, terrycot, jeans . . . I would love to wear jeans. So smart. Not for you, of course. Politicians can't wear jeans, no?

JEET (*laughs*). Imagine old man Thakur in jeans. But, seriously, I must get a good designer and tailor. That's something the men in the mountains didn't consider important. My mentor wore only an ankle-length kafni and a rudraksha string. Enough. No more chit-chat. Let's go. Find out from TOP if the car has gone to pick up Karan-ji.

PEON. Yes, sir.

*Jeet stands up. Peon whips out his mobile phone from his pocket and begins to press the buttons. Just then the song 'Maili Chadar' starts to play.*

JEET. It's Ma's song. Who's singing it?

PEON. An old sadhu. Beggar, actually. Many people know the song.

JEET. Give him a few coins, will you? And say shabash. And hurry.

PEON. Yes, sir. (*On the phone. Goes out from the other wing.*)

*Light slowly fades. Song continues, then fades.*

*Blackout.*

## ACT 3

### Prologue

*Bare stage. Peon enters front of stage.*

PEON. And so, 12 years passed. My boss grew older. Went from strength to strength. The constituency he began with is now in his pocket. He won the seat the first time, and then a second time too. No doubt, he will win it next time as well. In politics, the next time is never too far away. This time, he's making a bid for the top job. Chief minister, no less. The time for old men is over, he says. Unless you get young blood in the big chair, we will remain where we are.

In these 12 years, I have learnt a lot about politics. I have learnt that when you are at the bottom of the ladder, you are looking at the ground and all the creatures that walk on it. But as you climb, you start to see the clouds. My boss has now forgotten our days in the forest. He still remembers a few words of our language. He likes to greet me in our tongue when we are alone. But when Prince is with us, he doesn't even look at me. Not that I mind. It saves me from the need to give him constant attention. I use the spare time to educate myself. My boss used to have shelves full of books. All sorts. Books he read at college. Lots of Shakespeare. Books he read while he was away in the mountains. Dharmashastras, Puranas, Churchill, Hitler. He still reads those. Because he needs them for his speeches. The old ones have gone into a trunk. Those are the ones I read. Great stuff, I tell you. I didn't get Shakespeare at all. My boss' versions are all text-books, actually. Full of notes and glossaries. Prince doesn't read. He hasn't even been to college. He's like me. But he does have a lot of money. And a special kind of brain that's made for politics.

You haven't met Prince yet. You glimpsed him in the first act. Then he disappeared. But he's coming back. And how! Firmly established as my boss' right-hand man. A sort of sidekick. Chief chamcha. But

I see a glint in his eye that makes me wary. You never know when a chamcha will turn into a chhuri, leave the master crying: Et tu Brute! Anyway, because so many years have passed since we last met, I need to share with you a brief conversation I had with my boss after that first speech he made. You heard him practise it here. You also heard him ask me to give him my people's feedback. So here's him and here's me after the meeting. (*Acts out the conversation, playing both roles.*)

HE. So, what did they think?

ME. They loved it.

HE. Did they? They didn't clap.

ME. They're not used to clapping, sir. They just listen.

HE. So what did they hear?

ME. What you said.

HE. Stop stalling. I am asking you if there were any negative remarks. What did your great-grandfather say. He's a sharp one. He must have said something.

ME. Nothing, really.

HE. 'Nothing really'. He said something. Out with it.

ME (*laughing as if about to share a joke*). He said you never ran around naked beneath the trees.

HE (*laughs as if sharing the joke*). It's just a manner of speaking.

ME. I know.

HE. Yes, you do. But did you tell him? (*Getting a little angry*) Did you tell him that? That it's just a manner of speaking? Did you? Stupid old man. That's the trouble with you people. Don't want to come out of your jungle habits. You can go now.

PEON (*himself again*). Phew! You noticed my politics, didn't you? I didn't open my mouth. I let him rage. When in trouble, shut up. That's my motto. I didn't tell him my great-grandfather called him a liar. Every time I meet him now, he says, 'How's that liar?' Yes, of course, he's still alive. 105 and going strong. Doesn't give up, the old man. One more fight, he says. Then I'll go. (*Laughs till he weeps. Wipes his tears.*) So here we are. Into our third act. A quarter of a century after we began. Fasten your seat belts. We are about to take off.

**Scene 1**

*Lights come up. The TOP trio are seated on a settee. There is another settee and chair on the opposite side. And a stool in the corner. Peon walks in, greets the three men with folded hands, hands over some papers and sits on the stool. Prince walks in briskly, touches the feet of the trio and takes his place on the chair. Silence. Oak looks through the papers and passes them to Patel who glances through them and hands them over to Thadani. The silence continues. The three men fidget a little. Patel looks questioningly at Prince. Prince looks at Peon.*

PATEL (*to Peon*). Where is he?

PEON (*stands up*). Yes, sir?

PATEL. Where is your boss?

PEON. Puja.

PATEL. Does he know we're here?

PEON. You were expected.

PATEL. I said: does he know we are here?

PEON. He must.

PATEL. Isn't it your job to tell him?

PEON. No, sir. I'm not allowed to disturb him. (*Looks at his watch*) He'll be here in two-and-a-half minutes.

PATEL. You mean, he times his puja?

PEON. Yes, sir. He times everything. He is always on time. If you'll excuse me saying so, sir, you came five minutes earlier than expected.

THADANI. You've smartened up, haven't you?

PEON. In my position . . .

OAK. Your position? And what might that be?

PEON. CGTD. Chief of Getting Things Done. You pick up a lot when you're getting things done. If you don't smarten up . . . (*Gestures a cutting off of the neck. Hearing Jeet approach, he sits down again.*)

*Jeet enters, greets the three men with folded hands and sits at one end of the settee, his arm casually placed along its back. He is dressed in a deep-blue long-sleeved kurta, narrow cream-coloured pajamas and a long cream stole with a blue zari border, draped over the left shoulder, round the back and over the right arm. When he sits, he frees his right arm by laying the stole end in his lap. Silence. The three men shift about. Jeet crooks his finger at Peon. Peon bends his ear to Jeet's mouth. Jeet whispers. Peon goes out and returns with a file which he hands over to Jeet. Jeet puts it down beside him and places his arm on the back of the settee again.*

PEON (*goes right up to the three men and bends low*). Tea, sir? (*The three men look at each other and nod uncomfortably. Peon asks brightly*) The usual? Sugar and milk (*Patel nods*). Milk but no sugar (*Thadani nods*). No milk no sugar (*Oak nods*). I haven't forgotten, sir.

*The three men smile weakly. Jeet looks at his watch.*

PRINCE. You said you needed to meet Jeetendra Sinh-ji urgently.

OAK. Yes. But we were expecting a friendlier atmosphere. We're not the enemy, you know. The enemy is outside, at our doorstep. We came to alert you to its presence.

JEET. I've noticed. My eyes and ears are wide open, and I read the news.

THADANI. But you're still coddling those forest fellows. Making tall promises which will destroy the vision to which you have committed yourself.

JEET. I don't think you understand politics.

PATEL (*spluttering*). We don't understand politics? WE DON'T . . .

*A dog lets out a single bark within.*

JEET. QUIET, RAJA!

PRINCE. Mama-ji, he didn't mean that.

PATEL. You shut up. Let him tell us what he meant.

*The dog growls.*

JEET. Do I owe you that?

PATEL. You owe us an explanation of what you said to the business delegates who came to see you.

PRINCE (*picks up the file from the settee and walks over with it to the three men*). These are notes I made of the meeting.

OAK (*without touching the file*). We have seen those notes.

*Jeet and Prince exchange glances.*

JEET (*shifting a little*). We didn't send you the file.

OAK. No. Our bosses did. Yours and ours. They are worried.

JEET. Why?

OAK. Because these notes haven't assured them of what your real intentions are. If we want to be a developed state, we need business to come in. This (*shakes the file angrily*) gives no indication that you will welcome it.

JEET. So far, I have not been given any indication that I shall have the power to welcome it. Right now, all I have is this constituency. And to keep this constituency, I need what you refer to as those forest fellows. My words have kept them happy all these years. But with businessmen you have to talk brass tacks. Do I have the power to do so?

PATEL. So, you want our bosses to give you in writing that they will back you as Chief Minister?

PRINCE. He did not say so, Mama-ji.

PATEL. You shut up, you parrot. Let him tell us what he is saying.

*The dog barks. Peon enters with a tray, hiding his smile at what he has just heard. Hands a cup of tea to each of the three men and puts down a plate of biscuits on a side table.*

JEET. I am saying I need an assurance. An oral assurance from the Pramukh will do. A brief telephone conversation to say he has full faith in me and will back me.

THADANI. So, the Pramukh himself should call you and say . . .

JEET. Why? We will call him.

OAK. We?

JEET. I will call him myself.

OAK. I'm sure he would feel much obliged.

JEET. Or I will not call him, he will not call me, and I will continue to represent my constituency quite happily.

PRINCE. No, no. We will definitely call him. If you tell him in advance that this is what is worrying us.

OAK. Us?

PRINCE. Him.

OAK (*rising. The others rise too, Patel with some biscuit still in his mouth*). We shall write to the Upa-Pramukh about the conversation we have had. We will leave it to him and his Sahayyak Pramukhs to decide on the further course of action.

*They nod and leave.*

JEET. Good. That went well. (*Looks at his watch*) What time is your train?

PRINCE. In another hour.

JEET. You have to move.

PRINCE. Ji. (*Walks towards the wing*)

JEET (*to Peon*). What time is Karan-ji coming? (*Prince stops in his tracks as if he's forgotten something. Peon looks at him shrewdly*). Forgotten something?

PRINCE. No, no. I think I left my mobile . . . but you carry on. (*Peon is silent and so is Jeet. Prince pretends to look for his phone. Then touches his pocket and laughs*). It was here all the time. (*Walks swiftly away*)

JEET. Yes?

PEON. Four-thirty, sir. Sharmishtha-ji will also come.

JEET. Who decided that? (*Peon stands with bowed head*) Who said she could come? (*Holds out his mobile to Peon*) Call Karan. (*Stands up and starts to pace. Peon presses buttons, listens to the ringing at the other end and then holds out the phone.*) Who said Sharmishtha could come to see me? (*Listens*) She can't ride on your back. She should call me and ask. (*Listens.*) What could you have done? You could have told her the meeting was between you and me. (*Listens*) Of course there has to be some formality. (*Listens*) No. It is not old times. She cancelled old times long ago. She is telling those Vanvasis not to believe me. On what basis is she doing that? (*Listens. Lowering his voice*) No. We will not cancel the meeting. I want to see you. We haven't met for a long time. (*Listens*) Yes, I understand. Let her come. I don't have to take note of her. But if she says anything to upset me, there will be a fight. A big one. I wish you could dump her along the way somewhere. Never mind. I said, never mind. (*Listens*) Yes. Four-thirty. (*Disconnects and continues to pace up and down.*)

*Blackout.*

## Scene 2

*Peon rearranges the settees so that they are at right angles. Places the side table in front of them and takes out the single chair. As he returns, Karan and Sharmishtha enter. Peon greets them with real pleasure. Karan boxes him playfully on the chest and says, 'Hello, big man.' Sharmishtha takes his hand in hers. He leads them to a settee.*

SHARMISHTHA. You haven't been home in a while huh, Babu?

PEON. No time, sister. Parents dead. Sister gone away. Wife dead. Why come?

SHARMISHTHA. The old man is still alive.

*Peon's trained ears catch the sound of Jeet's footsteps.*

PEON. He's here. (*Goes to the wing. As Jeet enters, he touches his feet.*)

JEET. How many times must I tell you not to do that. (*Peon mutters and hangs back. Jeet walks over to Karan and gives him a big hug. Looks at Sharmishtha, smiles and nods*)

SHARMISHTHA. No hug for sister? (*Karan looks uncomfortable. But Jeet is suave.*)

JEET. Sure, if sister wants a hug. Though that's not part of our culture. (*Spreads out his arms but doesn't move forward. She comes to him. He lowers one arm and puts the other around her in a half hug. She sits down on the settee nearest to her. Peon gets up flustered because that's not where he had asked her to sit. Jeet signals to him not to worry and sits down beside Karan. Peon exits.*) How's college?

KARAN. As good as it can be.

JEET. Why, with you as head of faculty?

KARAN. The usual story. No funds.

JEET. Ah! Funds. How I hate that eternal sob story. I wonder if people say that in America. But give me a few years. We'll get rid of it. Rid of poverty. Stand shoulder to shoulder with America . . .

SHARMISHTHA. But until that happens, can we speak about poverty?

JEET. What's there to say about it?

SHARMISHTHA. Suyog needs funds. (*Pause. There's no reaction from Jeet*) I'm referring to the Sujata-Yogesh clinic set up by Baba and Ma.

JEET. Are you trying to put me down? I know what you were referring to.

SHARMISHTHA. I said that because I didn't see recognition on your face.

JEET. You didn't because I was waiting for you to tell me what I was supposed to do about it.

SHARMISHTHA. You've been telling us there's a big government-funded clinic coming up in Suyog's place?

JEET. There is.

SHARMISHTHA. So?

JEET. So?

SHARMISHTHA. So where is it?

JEET. You think these things happen overnight?

SHARMISHTHA. Ten years is overnight?

*The air crackles with tension. Peon walks in with a tea tray and sets it down on the side table. Hands over a cup of tea first to Jeet. Jeet waves towards Sharmishtha. Peon hands over a cup to her, then to Karan, then to Jeet.*

JEET. You're quiet, Karan. What do you have to say about this?

KARAN. About the clinic?

JEET. Yes.

KARAN. It needs funds.

JEET. She said that. About how long it takes to set up a large government-aided clinic?

KARAN. It depends on political will.

JEET. You mean *my* will.

KARAN. Your will if you think you have the power to set up such a thing.

JEET. That's what she doesn't see. Power is everything. I don't have that yet. When I do . . . and I will, I will . . .

SHARMISHTHA. Why promise when you don't have the power to redeem your word? It gives false hopes to people who are dying for lack of health care.

JEET (*stands up and starts to pace*). I promise, because I have a vision. A vision. It's something you lot lack. You can't see beyond the health of a few thousand people. I am thinking of the ultimate health of a country of 127 crore.

SHARMISHTHA. I may not think that big, Jeet (*Jeet squirms at the familiar name*), but I do believe that unless the health of every small thousand is assured, the larger 127 crore will never be healthy.

JEET. There is not a single nation in the world, not even America, where every single thousand is healthy. You discount the role genes play. The DNA.

SHARMISHTHA. I didn't express myself correctly. I should have said: where every thousand people have access to health care. And while I'm about it, let me add: where every thousand also has access to nutritious food to sustain itself.

JEET. Would your Vanvasis eat the food we offered? Would they not prefer their worms and frogs?

SHARMISHTHA. They might, if their worms and frogs were allowed to live. But they might grow to like other forms of protein too, if they were available and affordable. They might like fresh vegetables in addition to roots, if they were available and affordable. People's food habits change depending on what is available. And affordable.

JEET. You're taking off on your own flights of fancy now. My feet must remain on the ground. People can't and mustn't be served things on a plate. They must work for their food.

SHARMISHTHA. Are you, you of all people, telling me that our people don't work? Are you telling me that they aren't paid one-tenth of what your fat city men are paid for half that much work, most of which is simply sitting on their backsides?

JEET. I think I've had enough of this idle talk. Come into politics and see what it's like. Perhaps we'll say goodbye now. I've been waiting to talk to my friend here. I really don't have time to argue.

SHARMISHTHA (*standing up. Not angry. Nor bitter. Just matter-of-fact*). Thank you for giving me a hearing, Jeet. All I want for you is not to face a backlash. I still care about that.

JEET (*confused*). Thank you. I didn't mean for you to really go. Please wait. Let's talk without arguing. I have to thank you also for continuing to take care of Ma. I haven't seen her in . . .

SHARMISHTHA. She says it's 1 year and 39 days.

JEET. Trust her to keep count.

SHARMISHTHA. She's got only you.

JEET. She's got my adopted brother too. If she waited so many years to have a child, why did she have one at all? She's three generations behind me. It's so unfair. Such a burden.

SHARMISHTHA. It is, isn't it? To be the only child. To be given the freedom to do what you want . . .

JEET. I didn't have it laid out for me, I can tell you.

SHARMISHTHA (*had sat down, now stands up resolutely*). I'll tell Ma you're well and will visit soon. Is that the right thing to say?

*Jeet looks daggers at her.*

KARAN. I think it is. (*Looks at Jeet who nods noncommittally.*)

*Sharmishtha is walking out.*

JEET. And there would be no backlash if people weren't telling those idiots that I was lying to them. (*Sharmishtha turns, looks, smiles bitterly, shrugs and leaves*) Phew! Women! Good you've kept off them, dost. Wise. Very wise. That one you had at college . . .

KARAN (*smiles and does a mock sigh*). Sagari?

JEET. Yes. Most unusual name. And lived up to it. Went overseas to . . .

KARAN. . . . your dream place. America.

JEET. My dream place is here, Karan. Get that right. I shall create an America here. That's what I want to talk to you about. I'm taking off. In a couple of years, I'll be in the top seat. There will be health clinics everywhere. Glistening roads. Water for every farmer. And malls to beat any mall in America . . . Forget Singapore and Shanghai. That's all small fry. We are equal to the biggest. America. More than equal. We will have the money and the malls, but we'll also have our 5,000-year-old culture. We will force the world to acknowledge that we were once thinkers and inventers . . .

KARAN. Would you say WE were? Or would you say the Brahmin elite were?

JEET. Let's not bring caste into it, Karan. I've gone beyond that. When I say we, I mean every single person born on this sacred soil, whatever their caste or gender.

KARAN. Or religion? (*Pause*) The Adivasis are worried about their sacred grove. Suddenly there's movement around it. A road seems to be coming up. Too near to the grove for comfort.

JEET. What grove? What road? (*Karan looks at him but says nothing*) Of course I know the sacred grove. And why a road is coming up there. (*Long pause.*) Karan, please don't challenge me. We have been friends. I have no other. I am at a very difficult point in my career. It is touch and go. Rather, touch or go. There are moments when I feel absolutely alone. I need you Karan. You must stay by my side.

KARAN (*moved*). Nothing will budge me from your side.

JEET (*laughing*). That's what the TOP three are afraid of.

KARAN. What?

JEET. That you will never budge from my side.

KARAN. Oh? I worry them?

JEET. Of course you do.

KARAN. Me? Head of Humanities in a small college in a place nobody has heard of, lecturing on Plato, Bhartrhari and Chanakya to two students while dozens crowd the Commerce classes?

JEET. Yes, you. The men at TOP are afraid of your influence on me. They think the minute I'm in the top job, I will appoint you my right-hand man.

KARAN. And I will ditch my calling to answer your call?

JEET. They don't know how low your ambition is and how stubbornly you stick to your beliefs. I told them we are dreaming of a utopia. My friend is a poet. He knows poets get thrown out of utopias. He will never agree to become my official aide, however much I want it.

KARAN. If you want it.

JEET. I can't think of a time when I wouldn't.

KARAN. That time will come Jeet, when the only voice you'll want to hear is your own.

*Silence. 'Maili Chadar' is heard faintly in the distance, grows louder and passes on during the following dialogue.*

JEET (*thoughtfully*). Perhaps you're right. I must do this alone. Even one other voice might be one voice too many. A leader is like . . .

KARAN. Like?

JEET. . . . a god. Ancient cultures worshipped kings as gods. Gods don't have advisers.

KARAN. You said that to them? To Thadani, Oak and Patel?

JEET (*laughs*). No, no, no. They'd have written off to the Academy straightaway . . . (*Mimicking*) 'We would like to caution you about Jeetendra

Sinh-ji's ideas. He thinks he is God.' (*Laughs*) No, I told them you would never agree to be my aide but that you were the only man who had a place in my heart. (*Embarrassed at sounding sentimental. Changing his tone*) You are silent. Like the Sphinx.

KARAN. What is there to say, Jeet?

JEET. I have never known you to be lost for words. You must say what you think.

KARAN. Well . . . I don't really know . . . kings, gods . . . these are not ideas that we believe in now, do we?

JEET. Don't we? You must step out of your philosophy classes into the real world, Karan, and see and hear what real people believe. (*Watches him*) You are silent again.

KARAN. When I step out of my philosophy classes, I step into the Adivasi world. But that's not the real world that you are referring to. So, I must keep my counsel.

JEET. You are being sarcastic. It doesn't suit you, Karan. Do you really believe I don't have the best interests of our forest-dwellers at heart? That once I'm in power, I will not redeem every word I have given them in the last ten years?

KARAN (*long pause as he looks at Jeet with love and sympathy*). I want desperately to believe you will, Jeet.

JEET. To believe or not to believe is in your hands.

KARAN. If it were, I would believe in you straightaway. But it's a struggle. I'll say one thing, though, and say it with a clean conscience: I understand your struggle.

JEET. My struggle? There's no struggle. My path is clear. (*Peon enters almost on tiptoe and hands Jeet a small piece of paper*) My struggle is for time. Time to spend with you, with Ma. But (*waving the paper*) commitments call. My fat timekeeper, Prince, is waiting. (*Rising.*) We will go then, he and I . . . How does the real poem go? (*Karan rises.*)

*They walk towards the wing and halt.*

KARAN. Let us go then, you and I,
When the evening is spread out against the sky
Like a patient etherized upon a table;
Let us go, through certain half-deserted streets,
The muttering retreats
Of restless nights in one-night cheap hotels
And sawdust restaurants with oyster-shells:

*Jeet joins in.*

JEET. Streets that follow like a tedious argument
Of insidious intent
To lead you to an overwhelming question . . .
Oh, do not ask, 'What is it?'
Let us go and make our visit.
In the room the women come and go
Talking of Michelangelo.

*They laugh. They have entered another world. They hug. Karan exits. Jeet turns back and walks, still smiling, towards the other wing, reciting the last two lines of the poem. The stage is empty for a few seconds. The dog barks, then growls, then barks again. Peon hurries in to clear the tea things. Stands with the tray, looking towards the wing.*

PEON. There's a distinct chill in there. Not like the chill in the mountains that makes you shiver and your teeth chatter. This is different. It's a hot chill. Running up and down your spine even while you're fanning yourself. Talking about heat, old Great-grandpa is simmering in the village. Wants to come and see Jeet. Give him a talking-to. However much you grow in height, girth and status, for great-grandpas, you are still the snotty child who can be scolded. I've been trying to put off the old man, but do you think he'll listen to me? He isn't

Shakespeare's old man, 'Sans teeth, sans eyes, sans taste, sans everything'. He has four teeth left but they work, his eyes can see into the future, he still smacks his lips over a pungent frog, and as for sans everything—nothing doing. It's all in place, if you know what I mean. So, he'll come as soon as Jeet returns from his tour of the desert where he's just gone off with Prince to promise them water. I've tried to warn the old man about a few things here. He can still hear the rain coming over the hills, but he goes deaf when I tell him things. (*Shrugs.*) Fine. Let him find out for himself.

*Lights dim. Blackout.*

**Scene 3**

*The stage is bare except for one settee, a chair and Peon's stool. Jeet and Prince enter, talking. Prince stays two steps behind Jeet.*

JEET. That, I would say, was a success.

PRINCE. No doubt, no doubt.

JEET. A great success, I think.

PRINCE. I would say so.

JEET. They were eating out of my hands.

PRINCE. As they always do.

JEET. It's heady.

PRINCE. It is. Indeed, it is.

JEET. How would you know? (*Pause. Looks teasingly at Prince*) Unless you drink.

PRINCE. Sir, please, sir, you know I don't. I am like you. Strict teetotaller and vegetarian. Even my jokes.

JEET. You tell jokes, Prince?

PRINCE (*embarrassed*). Sometimes.

JEET. Tell me one. I'm in need of a laugh.

PRINCE. It's a little long.

JEET. That's all right. We have time before that pest of an old man comes.

PRINCE. You might not find it funny.

JEET. Try me. I'm in the mood to find many things funny. Come on, now. Don't be coy.

PRINCE. In Mumbai, a man is going to jump off a building. A good Hindu cop tries to talk him down: 'Don't jump! Think of your father.' The man replies, 'Haven't got a father—I'm going to jump.' The cop goes through a list of relatives: mother, brother, sister, uncle. Each time, the man says, 'I don't have one—I'm going to jump.' The desperate cop finally yells: 'Don't jump! Think of Krishna.' The man replies, 'Who's that?' The cop yells, 'Jump, you Muslim! You're blocking the traffic!' (*Looks uncertainly at Jeet. Jeet is looking around with an incipient smile on his lips. After he's sure that nobody's listening, he lets out a belly laugh, joined by a greatly relieved Prince.*)

JEET. You're not going to tell this joke to anyone else.

PRINCE. But already have. At my sister's wedding. They loved it.

JEET. Yes, well, why not. It's only a joke. You didn't mean harm.

PRINCE. Of course not.

*The dog begins to bark.*

JEET. I think Raja has smelt the old man.

PRINCE (*shouting*) Raja, shut up. Raja!

*Raja's barking is now added to by a chorus of street dogs.*

*Great-grandpa enters, escorted by Peon.*

PRINCE. I'll go and calm him down.

*The old man stands just inside the wing, looking into the opposite wing, waiting for the barking to stop. It doesn't. It grows more fierce. Jeet hurries forward and touches the old man's feet.*

OLD MAN. None of that. But gag that beast.

JEET. Sure. Won't you sit down? (*Points to the chair. To Peon*) What are you doing just standing there? Get Raja to calm down and bring the tea.

OLD MAN. You think I have come for tea? I've come to say just one thing . . . (*barking*), provided you can hear me.

JEET (*to Peon*). I thought I told you to shut him up.

*Peon exits with a backward look at the old man. The look says: Don't say I didn't warn you. Jeet sits down on the settee and signals to the old man to take the chair. The old man continues to stand and the dog continues to bark.*

OLD MAN (*shouting angrily above the barking*) They are building a road near our sacred grove.

JEET. Are they?

OLD MAN. You know they are.

JEET. Honestly, I don't. But I'll find out.

*The barking has stopped.*

OLD MAN (*lowering his voice*) You are lying, son. You shouldn't lie so much. Your father loved Gandhi. He never told a lie in his life. Every bone in his body was made of truth. Think of your father and never lie.

*Jeet has grown very stiff.*

JEET. I wasn't lying, Great-grandpa. Why would I lie to you of all people? I'll find out about the road.

OLD MAN. Don't try to fool me. You know what's happening in every bit of this place. It's your duty to know. But I'm not here to argue. I'm here to warn you. If that road goes through the sacred grove, there will be trouble. Big trouble.

JEET. Let me assure you, Grandpa. The road will not go through the sacred grove—it will go around it.

OLD MAN. To where?

JEET. I can't tell you that.

OLD MAN. Why not? We live in the forest. We worship in the forest. It is our land. Why should we not know what outsiders are planning to do in it?

JEET. Outsiders, Grandpa? We are all brothers, proud of this great nation aren't we? Your ancestors once defended it against the British.

OLD MAN. I don't know any nation. I know only the forest. Our ancestors fought for the forest. And since we are talking about them, I want to ask you something. You made a speech on the radio. All the villagers sat around to listen to you. In that long speech—how much you can talk, son—you spoke of national heroes. You spoke of Shivaji. You spoke of Maharana Pratap. But where were Tantya Bhil and Khajya Nayak and Birsa Munda? And you say *we* fought for the nation? We didn't. But we will fight for our forest. We will. Your dog is quiet. He agrees. (*Laughs with real amusement.*) Sometimes, animals are much more clever than us. (*Exit.*)

*Prince enters angrily, followed by Peon with tea.*

PRINCE. You shouldn't have allowed that bag of bones to . . .

JEET. Don't call him that. He is angry. Wouldn't you be too, if you thought your gods were about to be desecrated? I'll hold a meeting in the village one of these days. Tell them about the road. About the steel plant. And how it will benefit the people of the forest. Create jobs, health, education, food—for all of them.

PRINCE. They don't deserve any of those things, the barbarians.

*Silence as they sip their tea.*

JEET. I wouldn't say that. Everybody born on this soil deserves whatever we can do for them, without prejudice. That's what I was taught in the mountains. And I shall remain true to those teachings till the end of my days.

PRINCE. You are a good man and I am a loudmouth. Nothing will change that. (*Changing the subject*) I was wondering: should I visit Karan's college on Republic Day? They've organized a seminar. Karan has invited people from Delhi, Pune, even abroad, I hear. I wonder who's funded the jamboree. I'd like to hear all these people. We should know, shouldn't we? (*Jeet turns a wary eye on him*) Karan always has very stimulating things to say. Always a new angle on an old subject.

JEET (*still wary*). He does indeed.

PRINCE. So, shall I go?

JEET. It's for you to decide. I can't advise you on your every move, can I? (*His cup is empty.*)

*Peon hurries across to take it from him and place it on the tray. Then looks pointedly at Prince. Prince quickly swallows what remains in his cup and shifts in his seat. Jeet rises and begins to walk towards the wing. Prince follows two steps behind.*

PEON. Now what do you make of that? Does Jeet want Karan to be spied on? Or doesn't he? I think I know the answer. But I'll leave it to you to figure out.

## Scene 4

*The stage is arranged with two settees facing each other, a side table, a single chair and Peon's stool in the corner. Thadani, Oak and Patel are seated on one settee. Prince is on the chair. Jeet enters briskly with Peon following. Sits on the other settee, arranges his stole as before, crosses his legs, lays his arm along the back of the settee. Peon puts a file on the stool next to the settee, walks to his stool and sits down. Silence.*

OAK. Have you seen this report?

JEET. I see many reports. Which one are you referring to?

OAK. Prince's report. About the seminar at the university.

JEET (*glancing at the file on the side table*). I haven't had time to read it carefully. But I have glanced through it.

THADANI. That should be enough to give you an idea of what happened.

JEET. As far as I could make out, our youth stopped certain speeches from being made. That was as it should be. We didn't need to have this meeting to say that.

OAK. Obviously, we are here to say more than that. You don't have to be political with us. We are past masters at that.

JEET. All right, then. I'll be plain. The report indicts two speakers in particular. Sharmishtha and Karan. I've been through their speeches. They haven't said anything different from what they and others like them have been saying for a long, long time. That the Vanvasis and their lands have been exploited.

PATEL. Forget have been. *Are* being exploited. They spoke of the road.

JEET. They would, wouldn't they?

PATEL. They would. But should they? That's the question you have to answer Jeet . . . er . . . Jeetendra Sinh-ji. Should they, at a time when we are just one step away from achieving our goal in the region that we control? Our foot soldiers are already busy laying the ground. But we require funds. Those will only begin to flow if the right people believe in us. And—let us be frank. Our grapevine tells us the deep pockets are not at all sure about you.

JEET. I have done nothing so far to earn their distrust.

OAK. Haven't you? You're still in close touch with your old friends.

JEET. I have no friends. A leader can't afford to have friends. That is one of the first things we learnt at the Academy. Prince will remember.

PRINCE. Of course I do.

JEET. So why those implications in your report?

PRINCE. Not in my report. No. I would never do that.

JEET. No?

PRINCE. Ask them. It's not in the report. They were asking me about Karan and . . . and . . .

PATEL. Sharmishtha. So he told us they had come to see you. He wasn't there. So he didn't know what transpired. May we know?

JEET. No, you may not. They are old friends.

PATEL. And you spoke about old things? Only? Nothing else?

*Jeet is getting angry.*

OAK. We are not putting you in the dock. We believe in privacy.

THADANI. But only to an extent. We cannot compromise national security, can we?

JEET. I am as clear about that as anybody.

OAK. Then we are on the same page. Anybody who questions our policies which are meant to benefit the whole state, is acting against the state. Surely that's as clear as the noonday sun?

JEET. So?

THADANI. So this report makes it quite clear there are people among us who are acting against the state.

OAK. I had warned you about the enemy on our doorstep the last time we met. But there is also an enemy within. Unless we take care of that enemy, we cannot ensure the security of the state. That stands to reason. (*Jeet is silent*) You get our drift, don't you?

JEET. Yes, indeed I do.

THADANI. We trust you will make plans to ensure the state's safety?

JEET (*stands up*). I have never supported anything that endangers it.

OAK. That's all we wanted to hear.

*The three men rise.*

THADANI: You know that our foot soldiers are always ready to do your bidding. You just have to give the order.

JEET. I'll keep that in mind. (*The men are still unsure*) I think the meeting is over, don't you?

PATEL (*to Prince*). Come and see me later.

PRINCE (*embarrassed*). If saab doesn't need me.

JEET. No. Saab doesn't need you. You can go with them now if you like. (*He claps. Peon comes forward. Loudly, wanting the others to hear*) Call Karan-ji. Tell him I want him to come over as soon as he can. (*Looks at the four men*) Still here? Karan is an old friend. You know that. (*They exchange looks. Then leave. The dog barks. Turning to the wing*) You bark when they leave. When poor old grandpa came, you wouldn't let him speak. Where do you dogs learn such blatant discrimination from? You're not even a pure breed, just a mongrel. (*To Peon*) Have you called?

PEON. Ji, saab.

JEET. What did he say?

PEON. He's just finished class. He'll come. He also said . . .

JEET. What?

PEON. That he's famished. So could we give him something more than biscuits.

JEET. Give him hot puri-bhaji. I'll have only buttermilk.

PEON. Saab, full lunch is made.

JEET. I should hope so. But I'll have only buttermilk. (*Pause*) Tell me something. Why does this dog bark at poor people? I picked him up from the street. He used to eat off the garbage heap. But he barks at people who shared the garbage heap with him. How do you explain that?

PEON. It's hardly my place to comment, saab.

JEET. It is your place to comment because I'm asking you to comment. Your face tells me you have an answer to my question.

PEON. They call it aspiration.

JEET. Don't be silly. He's a dog.

PEON. He's an aspirational dog. In a democracy, everybody is allowed to have aspirations.

JEET. Would you say so?

PEON. Of course I would. But whether you can fulfil your aspirations depends on many things. Saab, this will take long to explain. I don't want to take up your time with my drivel.

JEET. Speak, man. I'm interested. I can't think of anything till Karan comes. Time hangs on my hands. I'd rather you filled it with your thoughts than I with mine. You were saying . . . ?

PEON. That everybody has a right to aspire. But you cannot fulfil your aspirations just because you have them. I don't think I'm being clear.

JEET. Then be clear.

PEON. I'll take an example. This dog. You call him Raja. It gives him ideas about himself. He wants to walk on his hind legs and sit on soft cushions. But he isn't equipped for it. So he seeks somebody who is less than himself. Somebody he can bully because he's frustrated, right? He doesn't want to be a dog. On the garbage heap, he was king over the two-legged wretches who shared it with him. Because he could sniff out the best pieces of garbage, and four feet were better to get to them than two. What does he do with all his angst here, where he is nothing but a dog with no garbage heap to prove he is king?

JEET. But why bark at your great-grandpa and not at the men who were just here?

PEON. Best not to say, saab.

JEET. No say. You must say. Go on.

PEON. I think he senses something in the air.

JEET. What?

PEON. Well, that some people have a right to be here and some don't.

JEET. But I touched the old man's feet.

PEON. So you did, saab. So you did.

JEET. Then?

PEON. He's just a stupid dog.

JEET. That's not what you were saying. You were saying he senses something in the air.

PEON. Pure drivel, saab. You should never give me a chance to talk. I know myself too well. I talk drivel.

KARAN (*enters laughing*). You talk drivel? Don't believe him, Jeet. This man of yours is a philosopher.

JEET. He is, he is. He was just lecturing me about democracy and people's aspirations.

PEON. No, saab. I never said people. I was only talking about dogs.

JEET. OK. Go get that food. We have a hungry stomach to fill here. (*Peon exits. Jeet indicates the settee to Karan while he sits on the chair. Karan is awkward. There's some 'no-no you must sit in your place' and 'how does it matter between friends' till they both settle down on the settee.*)

KARAN. What was Babu saying about dogs?

JEET. In a democracy, even dogs have the right to be aspirational.

KARAN. Really? That's deep.

JEET. He's a deep man. I haven't thought about democracy for a very long time. I must brush up on it. People bring it up all the time these days. Nothing we do seems to fit people's ideas about it. (*Thinking.*) I don't like it when you're silent. In the old days, you'd have challenged me.

KARAN. So far you haven't said a thing that I could challenge. You've only told me what Babu said.

JEET. Do you agree with that statement.

KARAN. Taken metaphorically?

JEET. Of course taken metaphorically.

KARAN. He's right.

JEET. I suppose he is. Our ancestors lived in simpler times. Each group of people could only be what they were. No aspirations beyond that. If you aspired, you sinned. Even Dronacharya sinned. Born a brahmin he did the work of a kshatriya. Just for the money and status.

KARAN. The only difference being that he wasn't punished for aspiring.

JEET. H'mm. So that's our chief problem, isn't it? So many groups with so many interests, all aspiring. How do you juggle? I believe you said something about democracy, justice and freedom in your talk at the university.

KARAN. It was hardly a talk. Just a philosophical statement of facts . . .

JEET. But citing America.

KARAN. You seem to know what I said. You weren't there.

JEET. Karan, are you really so naive? I don't have to be anywhere to know what people are saying or doing. (*Peon comes in with a plate of food for Karan and a glass of buttermilk for Jeet.*) Eat. Lecturing and arguing takes a lot out of a man.

KARAN. I could have had just buttermilk.

JEET. Atithidevo bhava.

KARAN. So I'm a guest now.

JEET. Anybody who comes to my door hungry is a guest.

KARAN. Especially when he has been summoned?

JEET. Did I summon you? (*Long pause*) I think we've got off to a wrong start. I think I've been riding the high horse a bit. I'm getting into the habit. It's not a bad habit. I need it for my work. But I must know when to get off that damned horse.

KARAN. Now that we're on a level, I don't mind eating while you drink plain buttermilk.

JEET. You're not so naive, after all. You also play power politics.

KARAN. (*his mouth full, he gesticulates*: '*Wait*'). I hope it's only to be equal. Not to have the upper hand. (*Continues to eat*)

JEET. You have it anyway. So, I want to know from the horse's mouth what the horse said at the university. I have a report with many implications. What I want is the ungarnished truth.

KARAN. The horse's mouth is rather full just now. Let me finish this. It's delicious. I rarely get hot food. (*Polishes off the food, washes it down with water, rises. Holds out his hands. Peon ushers him into the wing. He comes back, wiping his hands on a handkerchief*). Right. I'll tell you what I said. In Plato's *Republic*, Socrates and Thrasymachus have an argument about what is justice. I analysed it briefly for the audience because you know Socrates' method, don't you? It's one obvious sounding question after another leading you into a maze with an answer at the end.

JEET. Very tedious. Questions about issues that are essentially non-issues. I used to fall asleep.

KARAN. So I began by explaining the opposing positions that Thrasymachus the rhetorician and Socrates the truth-seeker take on the matter of justice. Gradually, Thrasymachus shifts his ground to avoid being pushed into a corner by Socrates. By the end, he has wittingly or unwittingly moved the debate from a definition of justice to a description of the ideal ruler. In the course of which, he appears to applaud a despot's devices, whether or not they do justice to his subjects. Using that point as a bridge, I shifted my own ground to 1858 and America and the difference of opinion between Abraham Lincoln and Stephen Douglas.

JEET (*caught up in Karan's ideas*). Who is Douglas?

KARAN. He was a US Senator who had once defeated Lincoln. Douglas argued that the southern states which wanted slavery should be free to decide the issue for themselves. That was the democratic thing to do. His position was called the doctrine of popular sovereignty. But, I reminded my listeners, however persuasive his argument was, we cannot forget that his support for it came from a consideration of personal material benefit. I went into details of that.

JEET. Which you will not divulge to me?

KARAN. Do you have the time? I could tell you. The details are very interesting

JEET (*looking at his watch*). You're right. I don't have the time. I could read up on it later. Fascinating. You're talking about the real world.

KARAN. I do that once in a while.

JEET (*laughing*). OK. So go on.

KARAN. Now Lincoln came from the opposite end, with the doctrine of natural right. Standing against Douglas' contention that whatever the people of a state or territory wanted made it right for them, and therefore right for democracy, Lincoln held that only a commitment to moral law could make a truly just society. He argued that equality was a self-evident truth enshrined in the American Declaration of Independence, and should provide the moral touchstone for the whole of the American republic. Douglas' affirmation of popular sovereignty was actually a statement of sheer power politics in which questions of justice were to be decided by the will of the majority.

JEET. Ah! That rings alarm bells. (*Thoughtful*) Yes. (*Pause*) Yes. I must think about this. (*Stands up and starts pacing*) I must think deeply about this. (*Looks at his watch*) But not now.

KARAN. You want me to go?

JEET. If you put it that way, yes. But if you'll allow me to be polite, I will say I need to rush now. I hope you don't mind.

KARAN (*standing up*). Not at all. I have some work myself.

JEET. I hope it's not some more plotting against us. (*Laughs bitterly*) Against the majority.

KARAN. Plotting? Me? I'm only a teacher of philosophy.

JEET. Teachers can be very dangerous.

KARAN (*spreading out his hands*). See? Unarmed.

JEET. Come on, Karan. We're both armed with the same weapon. Speech. Vacha. Saraswati dances on our tongues. On yours with her left foot. On mine with . . . I must admit . . . her right foot. See you soon, my friend. You are, as I have always said, a very fine human being. A better one perhaps than me. (*Embraces Karan. This embrace has an urgency about it that Karan finds puzzling. Jeet drops his arms and walks away without a backward look. Karan looks after him questioningly.*)

*Blackout.*

**Scene 5**

*Stage right is lit up. The rest of the stage is dark. Parts of it will light up later. The TOP table stands in the lit part with one chair at its head and two chairs on either side. Jeet sits at the head, Oak and Thadani on one side and Prince and Patel on the other. Peon sits on a stool close by. The men are sipping tea. Jeet beckons Peon who hastens forward with a file. Jeet takes out a bunch of clipped papers from it and distributes them to everyone.*

OAK (*reading the title page*). Desh Raksha Yojana (Vishpur Chunao Kshetra): National Security Plan (Vishpur Constituency). Looks good.

*Silence as they read and continue to sip their tea.*

JEET (*putting down his papers*). That's neat, though I say so myself. Very neat. I don't see a single weak joint in the plan. Foolproof. (*The others have also finished reading and there's a general glow on their faces.*) Right? Would you say this takes care of our problems . . . not at one go but one by one, as though by natural causes or reasons of justice? We can't rush things. We must be guarded. If fingers are pointed at us, we are dead. Of the many skills I was taught in the ashram, this one has been untested. Until now. And we shall pass the test. We will have to. There will be no second chance. (*His eyes have a hard glint perhaps because he is now wearing glasses.*)

OAK. We need to make 100 per cent sure of our facts before we set this plan in motion. This speech here. You say it is verbatim. How can we be sure of that?

PRINCE. It's not our . . .

*Jeet raises a finger. Prince looks apologetic and shuts up.*

JEET. You don't need to trust our words. All you need to do is trust technology. (*Nods to Peon who carries in a small casket and places it before Jeet.*) When you see what comes out of this, you will think I'm being funny. But I'm not. (*Opens the casket and reverently draws out a smartphone*) This is a smartphone. Because it is smart. It's magical. The old mobile which we got in '95 before I left for the leadership course can now go into a museum. This one records, shoots pictures, videos. Let me show you. (*Holds the phone up, shoots a selfie and passes it around.*) It's the first one in the market. I'd been reading about it. I was looking out for it. And here it is. I had to enshrine it in this. After all, it is going to win us the campaign. Now, listen. Check it out with what's on that sheet.

SHARMISHTHA'S VOICE. We have our Sun God, our Hill God, our Rain God, our Earth Spirit. If we wish to preserve our gods and our way of life, we must pray to another god that these modern times have given us. That god is called Democracy. She is a good god if you understand her powers. You do not see her coming down as rain or shining on us like the sun. Her powers are written down in a big book called the Constitution. The only way we can preserve what we have is by knowing her rules and using them. We suffered under our white rulers because there was no Constitution. But when they were driven away, some good men wrote the Constitution which gave us equal rights with the rich. By and by, because of our fight, we won ownership rights to our forests. They appointed people called governors who had the power to prevent people grabbing our land. But no governor has ever done his duty by us. They talk of needing our land for development. What is this development? It is about cutting our trees and digging into Mother Earth, to take out her riches by blasting, exploding, hammering. Without our permission. We are not selfish. We could talk to them about what they want and what we want. We could agree to parts of the forest being used for development. Don't we have gram sabhas to decide our problems? We would like those outsiders to talk to our gram sabhas. If they don't, we will have to fight. We have fought many battles before. We must remember Tantya Bhil and Birsa Munda. But also Mahatma Gandhi who was Baba's hero. He too fought but not with bows and arrows. He fought peacefully. We will remember all these great men. From them we will draw strength to fight. Praise be to Baradeo.

PATEL. Who is this Baradeo?

PRINCE. Their Bhagwan. Creator of the World.

THADANI. It's her voice, all right.

OAK. Inciting the people.

THADANI. Against the state.

OAK. That is sedition.

THADANI. It is. It is definitely sedition. You're right, Jeetendra Sinh-ji. Absolutely right. We must take action against her.

PATEL. Once she is removed, the other part of the plan can kick in, right, Jeetendra Sinh-ji?

JEET. It is all there. Ready for action. It is now up to you to see it through. Will this loosen the purse strings of the steel men, the manganese men, the coal men?

PATEL. It will. It must. They need us as much as we need them. Another round of chai? (*He claps. Peon exits.*)

PATEL. There's one fly left in the ointment. (*Looks around the table. They look warily at Jeet. Jeet ignores them.*) You haven't addressed yourself to the danger it holds.

OAK. Jeetendra Sinh-ji, we need to settle that doubt.

THADANI. An assurance, really, that we needn't worry.

PATEL. I hope you are listening, Jeetendra Sinh-ji.

JEET. I am.

PATEL. We are talking about your friend Karan.

JEET. What about him?

PATEL. He is going to every university seminar in the country and talking about justice and democracy.

JEET. Yes, I know. So?

OAK. Look, Jeetendra Sinh-ji. Let us take it step by step. We are a free country, aren't we?

*Peon enters with tea and serves them all. Then returns to his place.*

JEET. I don't like the Socratic method of questioning that pushes people into corners. I'm not as stupid as some of the old Greek philosophers appeared to have been. Let's talk man to man. Karan is invited by universities to talk because he is a man with an uncommonly clear, bright mind and a way of articulating complex ideas in an accessible way. That makes him the darling of intellectuals and students alike. Are we holding his popularity against him?

OAK. Certainly not. We are holding his ideas against him.

JEET. He speaks about justice and democracy. Don't we believe in those values?

OAK. Of course we do. But you know as well as we that to speak of justice and democracy in a just and democratic society is to imply they don't exist here. That creates disaffection among people against the elected rulers of the state. Do we allow this to continue?

JEET. I hope you realize you are asking a fundamental question? You are asking whether we do or do not allow people to express their ideas freely? Are we against free speech?

OAK. Only if it endangers the state.

JEET. So, there's your answer. Karan isn't inciting people to rise and fight. Therefore, he is not endangering the state.

PATEL. It appears you haven't heard him speak.

JEET. Not in person. But he has told me what he has been saying and I trust him implicitly.

PATEL. You think he's saying the same thing wherever he goes?

JEET. More or less. How much more is there to say about justice and democracy as philosophical ideas?

THADANI. I think we'll do what we had planned to do anyway.

JEET. Which is?

THADANI. Send our boys to one of his lectures and record it as you have done. Just to make sure.

JEET. As you please. You will find nothing incriminating. (*He rises. Peon clears the tea things. Prince stands up as well. Jeet and Peon exit. The others restore the table and chairs to their usual positions and take their seats with Prince in the visitor's chair. Oak begins to speak as the light dims. It comes up stage left. Jeet enters, followed by Peon. Jeet is on the phone.*) I don't have time for an argument, Karan. I want to know just one thing. Have you been speaking against the state? Stop joking. I want a straight answer. You know what I'm implying, don't you? Answer with that in mind. No? Sure? Are you corrupting young minds as your favourite philosopher Socrates once did? That's the charge against you. Of course you aren't going to be arraigned and offered hemlock. But, as my friend, would you mind not accepting any invitations for the next six months while I'm campaigning for the elections? It's a tricky time for me, Karan. No. It's not enough to say you have no engagements for the next six months. You need to say you will not accept any engagements till the elections are over. Say it again. Once more. Good. Thank you. Thank you very much. That takes a load off my chest.

*Lights fade and come up centre stage, casting a shadowy light on prison bars. Three policemen, played by Oak, Thadani and Patel, bring in Sharmishtha, handcuffed, from centre back, and throw her to the floor of the prison cell. They dust their hands and saunter to front stage.*

SHARMISHTHA (*stands up, eyes blazing*). You will not win. Even if I rot in this prison, you will not win. (*The policemen turn, then face front, their faces expressionless.*) Human rights are sacred in a democracy. Any fight for rights is a just fight. Our people will fight that fight. (*The policemen make to leave. She raises her voice.*) And do me a favour. Tell your boss, now that he has put me in prison, he must arrange for the woman who gave him birth, to be cared for. She is old. She is old and sad and ill. Tell him that, do you hear?

*They exit. Light dims on that part of the stage and comes up again stage left where Jeet is pacing.*

JEET (*beckons Peon*). I want you to go to your village. I am told Sharmishtha-ji has been arrested. The villagers must be very disturbed. Calm them. Tell them I'll come and explain everything to them. The police say it is only for a short time. Just to teach her a lesson. Talk to your great-grandpa. Will you do that?

PEON (*hooded eyes*). I will try, saab. But Great-grandpa is a stubborn old fellow. He remembers too much tribal history. He doesn't even acknowledge me as kin. He says I have sold out.

JEET. Tell him you haven't. Your roots are still there. You must convince him about that.

PEON. I will try, saab. I will try.

*'Maili Chadar' plays in the distance.*

JEET. And send Prince-saab in if he's back from his intrigues in the TOP office.

PEON. Yes, sir. (*Exit*)

*Prince enters, a bit flustered.*

PRINCE. I knew you'd send for me. I didn't believe you wanted to have this meeting without me. Have they come? It is the most important meeting, strategically speaking. I'm glad you've had second thoughts.

JEET. No, Prince. I never have second thoughts. I don't want you to be present. I want you to go out there and make sure that that sadhu or fakir or whoever he is never comes this way singing that song. He irritates me intensely.

PRINCE. Can't hear anything. (*The sadhu's voice comes closer*) Oh, that one? That's your mother's favourite bhajan isn't it?

JEET. Can we have action instead of words?

PRINCE. Certainly. As soon as our visitors have gone.

JEET. No, now. I will take care of our visitors.

*The voice is very close.*

PRINCE. As you say, saab. I'll put the boys on to it. (*Leaves, pressing the buttons on his phone. A little later, the sadhu's voice stops. Prince returns.*) Job done. Voice silenced forever.

JEET (*shocked*). Forever?

PRINCE. Isn't that what you meant? Or wanted? (*Watches Jeet shrewdly. Jeet turns away*) Anyway, who's going to miss an old sadhu? No use leaving things half-done. (*Laughs.*)

JEET. You may go now.

PRINCE. Go?

JEET. Yes, go.

PRINCE. You mean you don't need me? The visitors are businessmen. I'm good at deals. It's in my blood.

JEET. I am well aware of the skills in your blood, Prince, and I appreciate them deeply. But it isn't time for deals yet. When the time comes, you'll be the man in charge. I'm not interested in the spinoffs that come with deals. I am only looking for funds for the campaign.

PRINCE. What spinoffs? I'm working for the nation. Not for myself.

JEET. Yes, of course you are. But, as I said, I don't need you at this moment.

PRINCE (*about to look disgruntled, quickly changes expression to look submissive instead*). Sure. Sure. I see your point. (*Exit*)

*Three businessmen in sharp suits enter, played by Oak, Thadani and Patel. They bow obsequiously to Jeet. Jeet bows obsequiously to them. They sit down. Momentary silence.*

OAK. We believe all arrangements have been made to clear the ground for the plant? We hope the road will be complete before the rains? Our trucks will start moving in as soon as the monsoon is over.

JEET. Everything is on schedule. May we trust you to keep your word about the funds?

THADANI. We never go back on our word. You need not doubt us.

JEET. Doubts come without my willing them. This is Kali Yuga, gentlemen, not Treta Yuga. None of us is Harishchandra. I suggest we sign an MOU next week in which we will state our promises and you will state what you will give in return. We'll arrange for the signing in the TOP office. After we've consulted our respective lawyers and finalized the agreement draft.

OAK. Suits us. Once that's done, we can get on with plans for the Bhumi Puja. By then, the elections will be over. You will be in the chair . . .

JEET (*fearful, with urgency*). Stop. It's inauspicious to say it. Take back what you said.

OAK. All I meant was that, after the election dust has settled, you will be in a position to strike the ceremonial first blow on the site of the plant. (*Rubs his hands in glee.*)

*The three men beam at each other.*

PATEL. It is a very exciting time for the country. Riches will begin to flow when those blast furnaces get going. It will be a new life for the locals. Their labour will translate into lives they haven't dared to even dream of. It's a win-win situation for all.

THADANI (*looking doubtfully at Jeet*). Gandhi warned against greed. So do our holy books. We are fully aware of the danger of greed taking over. (*To the others*) Right?

OAK. Oh, yes. But we also know that we can't swallow what the holy books say hook, line and sinker. Fundamental principles are eternal. Details change with time. The great Mahabharata war was OK for its times. There was no business activity then. But today we don't need a war to disrupt business. Even a prolonged agitation affects business. We are told you have taken steps to pre-empt such disruptions.

JEET (*stiffly*). Yes we have.

THADANI. You will ensure that we will be able to conduct our business in peace.

JEET. Yes. Peace is as necessary for politics as it is for business.

PATEL. That is reassuring to hear. Perhaps we should take our leave now?

JEET (*rising*). Thank you very much for coming. It was necessary for doubts to be cleared on both sides. (*Hands are shaken all round. The three men leave. The phone rings. Jeet answers*) Yes? Oh, it's you? Yes, of course I've read the news. What do you mean I've imprisoned her? Sorry. I had nothing to do with it, Karan, nothing. The police heard a speech of hers and thought it was seditious. So they arrested her. We live in a democracy, Karan. The law is independent of the executive. You laugh. You find that funny. But it isn't. The state is being threatened from outside. We can't afford to have an enemy inside too. I know I'm not the prime minister. Not even a chief minister. Yet. But when I am, and I will be, I will be, I will always allow the law to take its course. What? But you gave me your word you wouldn't. Fine if you feel that way. But don't use it as a threat. It doesn't scare me. I've grown strong, Karan. I don't care what you or anybody else says. I am committed to the welfare of the state, the country. I will not have you or anybody standing in the way of my fulfilling my destiny. Yes. I am talking big. I do see it as my destiny. It IS my destiny. Fine. Go ahead. Do what you think you must. And goodbye. You are going back on your word. You weren't going to open your mouth till after the elections. You are betraying me. You are betraying our friendship. Right. So this is goodbye. Forever, Karan. Forever. (*Switches off his phone. Stands in shock at what has happened.*)

*Lights fade. Blackout.*

### Scene 6

*The stage is bare except for smoke drifting in from the wing. A havan is in progress. Mantras on the soundtrack. Peon in his place. Karan rushes in.*

KARAN. Where is he? (*Peon signals to the wing*) Tell him it's urgent.

PEON. Can't. He is praying for victory. Can't be interrupted.

KARAN. But he must. Ma is dying.

PEON. What?

KARAN. He must come.

PEON. Shall I tell him?

KARAN. You must. She's asking for him. (*Peon moves gingerly into the wing. Karan paces. Peon returns, shaking his head.*) What did he say?

PEON. Nothing.

KARAN. What did you tell him?

PEON. I said: Ma is dying. She's calling you.

KARAN. And?

PEON. He opened his eyes and put ghee on the fire.

*Karan is horrified. He rushes out. Lights fade and come up in the corner where Ma is on her cot. Stertorous breathing. In-between, she calls out 'Jeet' in a faint voice. Karan rushes in.*

MA (*turning her head*). Jeet?

KARAN. He's coming, Ma. He's coming.

MA. He must be busy.

KARAN. Yes. Very busy. But he'll come. He's coming. (*Sits on the floor holding her hand. Peon enters. Karan looks at him. Peon shakes his head. To Ma*) You remember, Babu? The old man's great-grandson?

*Ma turns her head and smiles. Peon swallows a sob.*

KARAN. He says Jeet'll be here any minute. You'll see him, Ma. You'll see him.

MA. I, I . . . There's no time. I'm going. Tell him I forgive him. I bless him. He has his father's blood in him. He won't betray it. He will . . . he will . . .

KARAN (*looks at Peon, his face ashen.*) Call the doctor. I think she's gone. (*Peon rushes out. Karan sobs uncontrollably.*)

*Jeet strides in. Takes in the scene. Sits on Ma's cot and sobs.*

JEET. When?

KARAN. Two minutes ago.

JEET. I wish she had waited. (*Looks at Ma*) What did she say?

KARAN. Nothing except 'Jeet'.

JEET. Nothing? Don't hold out on me, Karan. You were here. I want to hear every detail.

KARAN. What detail? I saw she was on her way out. I said I'll get the doctor. She said: No beta, it's no use. Get Jeet. I want to see him before I go. (*Jeet swallows, wipes his eyes*) I ran over to your place. You were busy.

JEET. Don't say it that way. I WAS busy.

KARAN. I was there. I saw you were busy. I ran back and told Ma you were coming. But she was just a few minutes from the end. The last thing she said was she forgave you. She blessed you. You had your father's blood in you. You would not betray it.

JEET (*rising*). Poor woman. I'm glad she went with her illusions intact.

KARAN. Illusions?

JEET. Yes, illusions. But she was pretending. She wasn't a fool. She knew I had rejected my father's blood. After a long, long fight. The old blood had to be drained out of me before fresh blood could be pumped in. (*Stands thinking.*) Thank you, Karan, for being there. You did all you could. Can I say . . . will it sound false . . . if I said I shocked myself the other day when I spoke to you on the phone? I was angry. Very angry. But when I calmed down, I saw there could never be a final goodbye between us. Karan, don't hold the things I said against me.

KARAN. I don't. You've chosen a difficult path and I understand.

JEET. Do you also forgive me?

KARAN. Why ask? If I don't hold what happened against you, what is there to forgive?

*Jeet holds out his hands. Karan takes them in his own.*

JEET. May I be alone with Ma now, please? I want to make a last bid to explain myself to her. (*Karan's face is a question mark*) There is a theory that a person continues to hear and feel for a few hours after death.

KARAN. I'll leave.

JEET. And be yourself, Karan. I need you to be yourself. You must say what you must. Do what you must. If you don't, you will not be Karan. And then, perhaps, I will not be Jeet. (*Karan leaves. Jeet stands there, looking down at Ma.*) I hope desperately that you can hear me, Ma. I want you to understand that a leader cannot afford to be vulnerable. Love and compassion weaken him. I am fighting the weakness I inherited from you. I haven't succeeded yet. But I will. I must. Ma, people loved you and Baba. But I don't want to be loved—I want to be feared. Some say my eyes have grown cold. I am happy if they have. But there is still too great a distance between my eyes and my heart. I need to destroy that distance. If cruelty is demanded of me, I must have the strength to be cruel. One act of cruelty is enough to clear the road for doing good. It puts a permanent fear into people. To do good in this country Ma, this poor, suffering country, we need to overturn the very order of things. That is my ultimate aim, Ma. To pull this country forward towards a radiant future while holding on to its ancient past. It is a feat no other world leader has had to attempt. But that is my vision. Ma, you didn't believe in my vision. You didn't see the sun that I saw. You named me Jeet, but you didn't think I could or even should conquer the world. And yet . . . (*He kneels by the cot. 'Maili chadar' plays, first softly, then a little louder.*)

. . . and yet I know you loved me. You forgave me. You blessed me. I weep at the goodness of your heart. You are now on your way to your rightful place. You often sang a song that was not for you to sing. You go as unblemished as you came. I hear the song often in my head. One day, I hope to stop hearing it. I cannot afford to look back on Baba, you, your song. I am concerned now with the future. If I realize my vision, history will applaud me. Every stain on my shawl will be washed away. God will forgive me. If I fail . . . (*He rises, facing the exit*) But I will not fail. I am destined not to fail. Do you hear me, you forest dwellers out there? I have given up much and will give up more. All for you. I have made my choice. The path before me is clear. Do you want to go with me or stay where you are with your sentimental philosopher-poet? The choice is yours.

# ACT 4

## Scene 1

*Three months have elapsed since Ma's death. Jeet has been campaigning day and night. He enters, looking very tired.*

JEET. Prince. Prince. Where are you? Where's our man? Where is everybody? (*Tries to call various numbers on his phone. Doesn't get through. Paces. Tries to call again. Gets through.*) What the hell's going on here? Mr Patel, is Prince with you? So where is he? What is that supposed to mean? Of course I know he has jobs to do. I'm the one that gives him the jobs. And I haven't given him any. So where is he? I demand to know. Wait? Wait? I MUST WAIT? That is a very strange request to make. Here I am trudging from one chamber of commerce to another, addressing men with eyes of steel and fingers that don't stop counting. And while I'm away, my people are off gallivanting . . . no they aren't? So where are they? Where is Prince? What? Oak is waiting to speak to you? No, I will not hold on. Tell him to speak to me. I need Prince here. This minute. Or else . . . (*Switches off the phone. Very scared*) Or else what? Someone is stabbing me in the back. I knew it would happen one day. I was prepared for it. But not now. Not so soon. I have been caught off guard. (*Paces*) I need to stop this evil. Nip it in the bud. (*Paces*) I need priests. (*Pulls phone out of his pocket. Presses buttons.*) Hello. Swamiji. Swamiji, can you hear me? What's all that noise? Can you step out where you can hear me? This is urgent. I want you here. Yes. Now. Bring your brother, uncle, anybody. I need three, with good strong voices. I heard you. I get it. I SAID I GET IT. It's a family occasion. You are naming your grandson. Yes, yes. You're naming him . . . What? Jeet? Great. But name him afterwards. There's a national crisis here. That's more urgent than naming grandsons. LISTEN, SWAMIJI. You are being paid big money for keeping the nation safe. COME AND DO YOUR JOB.

Yes. Now. (*Stuffs the phone back in his pocket and flings himself down on the settee, head in his hands. A faint crackling sound begins in the distance. He springs up and wheels around. A slow glow spreads on the cyclorama followed by a huge explosion. Three priests hurry in: Thadani, Oak, Patel.*)

OAK. Jai Shri Ram.

JEET (*urgently*). Hanuman mantra. Loud and clear. A thousand times. Yes. A thousand times. You can see what's happening out there, can't you? It won't take more than ten minutes the way you chaps garble the words. GO.

*Priests hurry in. The chanting begins. The crackling intensifies and mingles with the chanting. Jeet watches the glow, transfixed. There is an explosion. The cyclorama bursts into orange, bathing Jeet's face in an unholy light. Prince hurries in carrying pieces of coconut on a plate, his face glowing with triumph.*

PRINCE. We've done it.

JEET. Done what?

PRINCE. Carried out the plan. Cleared the road for the steel plant.

JEET. You mean you . . . who gave you the orders? Who said you could . . .

PRINCE. There was no time for could and should. We had to decide fast.

JEET. We?

PRINCE. At TOP.

JEET. Since when did they . . .

PRINCE. Someone had to decide. You were giving speeches . . .

JEET. Excuse me. I am fighting an election.

PRINCE. Sorry, saab. I'm bad at words. But you were away and things were happening.

JEET. Such as?

PRINCE (*pointing to the back*). There was a flash agitation. The villagers marched. No slogans. Just hundreds of them, marching. Our moles informed us. We came to a quick decision. They were on their way to the sacred grove. They were going to squat there. Satyagraha. We already had our plan in case they did some such thing, hadn't we? It was all in our plan. TOP decided this was the moment to put it into action. We had already parked our jeeps with explosives on the road to the grove. Our boys did the rest. (*Points jubilantly to the cyclorama.*) The villagers will either run for their lives or stay and . . . well . . . It is April. The trees are dry . . . (*Proffers the plate in his hand.*) Prasad. This was quick thinking by the boys. They had the coconut with them. Imagine. They brought it along. Threw it into the first flames. Like Holi.

*Jeet picks a piece of coconut absently. Puts it in his mouth. The mantras stop. The priests enter. Prince offers them the prasad. They linger. Prince looks at Jeet. Jeet nods absently. Prince pulls some money out of his pocket and offers it to them. Patel takes it.*

JEET (*absently*). Thank you. Thank you for coming. Hanuman has answered our prayers. (*The three priests hurry away. Long pause. Speaking very slowly and precisely*) Was Karan there?

PRINCE. Where?

JEET. With the villagers.

PRINCE. How would I know?

JEET. The way you knew about the agitation. Was Karan leading it? (*Shouting*) Was he in the sacred grove with the villagers, Prince?

PRINCE. Yes.

JEET. Leave me alone.

PRINCE. Saab?

JEET. Are you deaf? Leave me alone.

PRINCE. Yes, saab (*Hurries away.*)

*Light on Jeet fades. It comes up on the prison bars at the back.*

SHARMISHTHA. I didn't know you would stoop so low, Jeet. I didn't think you had lost every shred of humanity. You are evil. You know what the sacred grove means to them. They are stubborn. They are there even now as the flames lick around trees that have stood there for hundreds of years. They would rather go with the grove than live without it, Jeet. That makes you a murderer. You have nursed a violent rage against invaders who ruled hundreds of years ago because they destroyed your temples and desecrated your idols. And yet you thought nothing of destroying what was sacred to our own people. (*Long pause.*) I had thought however evil you were, you were sharp enough to work in your long-term self-interest. For a few crore rupees more, you could have bypassed the grove to build the road. You could have lived off that political capital all your life. But the devil is often short-sighted and stupid besides being evil. I pity you Jeet. Forget Ma and Baba—you have let yourself down.

*Light on the cyclorama remains as the stage grows dark. That glow is to remain till the end of the play.*

## Scene 2

*The distant sound of drums and pipes. The music grows louder. The lights come up as the music reaches a crescendo. Jeet enters, tousled and sweaty. Around his neck hang a dozen garlands. Prince follows him, grinning. A new Peon, played by the old one, follows, his arms loaded with more garlands.*

PRINCE. The counting will continue for hours, but we have won. Haan, Jeetendra Sinh-ji? We have done it. We have won. You are Chief Minister of the largest and most important state in the country, the home of warriors and wealth, saints and statesmen, the ferocious lion and the hardy camel. The land of river and ocean, hill and valley, forest and desert. The land with iron in its womb. We have it all. And now we have a great ruler. A man of iron, a saint and a statesman, a warrior and a lion all rolled into one. It was just such a ruler that this wretched land was waiting for, to deliver it from the stinking sludge of poverty into the golden light of the sun, like a new-born lotus. Hail to you our saviour! All hail!

*Voices from outside cry 'Jai Jeetendra Sinh-ji. Jai Jai Jai!' The music stops. Cries of 'A speech a speech!' Raja's happy whimpering.*

JEET. You make the speech, Prince. You have already waxed poetic. You're in the mood. Do it.

PRINCE (*bashfully*). Me?

JEET. Yes, you. You'd better get used to making speeches. You're going to be my right-hand man.

PRINCE. I'll try. But it isn't me they want to hear. It's you.

JEET. All right, then. Make a speech anyway and say I'm coming. I must spend a little time with Raja. (*They exit from opposite sides.*)

*Peon, who has been standing by patiently, lays down his armful of garlands on the settee. Prince's voice from outside: 'Oh you lucky people. Do you even know what you have done? You have elected the greatest ruler that has ever existed on earth. A man of iron. (Peon leaves the stage) A saint and a statesman, a warrior and a lion all rolled into one. It was such a ruler that this land was waiting for in its wretchedness—' (The speech stops abruptly. Poem returns.)*

PEON. You don't really want to hear him, do you? You're going to hear the same shit for the next five years. I switched off his mike. Peons have a lot of opportunities to be useful if they're alert and rise to the occasion. The chap who was here before me gave me tips. I come from the same village. Also Twelfth pass. The old chap told me about

SWOT—Strengths, Weaknesses, Opportunities, Threats. But I'm smarter. I won't let delicious opportunities slip through my fingers. Shutting Fatty off was one of them. Power fails in these parts all the time. Let's say this is one of those occasions. Oh, oh! Here they come. I call them POT. Just to myself. Turn TOP around and you get POT. (*Makes a zip-the-lip gesture and walks back to his stool.*)

*Enter Thadani, Oak and Patel with a new spring in their steps, each carrying a parcel. They sit down in their usual places with their parcels in their laps.*

THADANI (*to Peon*). Who are you? Where's the other fellow?

PEON. Ji, saab?

THADANI. The man who used to be here.

PEON. Don't know, saab.

PATEL. How can that be? You look like a Vanvasi. He was also a Vanvasi.

PEON. Yes, saab.

PATEL. So you should know him.

PEON. What was his name? Which village was he from?

OAK. You expect us to know that? Forget it. Is your boss back?

PEON. Yes, sir.

THADANI. Where is he?

PEON. Spending quality time with the dog.

THADANI. Dog?

PEON. Raja. He is very happy.

PATEL. The dog is happy? Useless fellow. Does he ever bark?

PEON. Oh yes, saab. He barks at me.

*Raja is making happy sounds. Jeet's voice, 'Raja, that's enough. Enough. Don't put your paws on me, you stupid mutt. I've just changed.' Peon hears a footfall and rushes to the wing. Jeet walks in majestically, wearing a deep-purple shirt-sleeved kurta, cream straight pajamas and a cream stole with a purple zari border. Peon bends to touch his feet.*

JEET. How many times must I tell you not to do that. (*Hurries forward to touch the three men's feet. They bless him.*) And where's Prince?

PEON. Trying to bring the power back.

JEET. What's wrong with the power?

PEON. It failed while he was making a speech.

JEET. Really? But it hasn't failed in here.

PEON. Yes, saab.

JEET. Strange.

PEON. Yes, saab.

*Thadani, Oak and Patel have opened their parcels ceremoniously.*

OAK. Sit down, Jeetendra Sinh-ji, sit down.

*Jeet sits, looking questioningly at the three men who are beaming. Oak places a crown on Jeet's head, a replica of the one he received as TOP's Young Leader. Then Thadani drapes a rich shawl round his shoulders.*

PATEL (*holding up a replica of the pugdee that Karan had won*). And where's my nephew?

JEET (*wary*). He's trying to make a speech.

PATEL. He can't make speeches.

JEET. He's learning. Why?

*Prince enters, very flustered.*

PATEL (*holding up the pugdee*). This is for him.

JEET (*suddenly cold*). No, it is not. (*Takes the pugdee from Patel and sets it down on the settee.*) *This* is for him. (*Takes the shawl from around his shoulders and hands it over to Patel.*)

*Awkward silence.*

PATEL (*hastily*). Yes, of course. Much more appropriate. (*Puts the shawl round Prince's shoulders*) Congratulations, son. You have won.

PRINCE. Damned power failed.

PATEL. I said: Congratulations. You have won.

PRINCE (*obsequious*) Not me. Saab has won.

PATEL. Don't be literal. Actually, I should say WE have won. We've all worked for this day. Come here. You haven't touched our feet. (*Prince rushes forward and touches the three men's feet. They settle down in their usual places, Prince on his chair.*) Where's the other chap?

JEET. Which other chap?

PATEL. The man who went with you to the Academy. The one you stole from us.

*They all laugh.*

JEET. Oh, him? He's run away.

PATEL. Never trust them. I don't suppose he told you he was going?

JEET. He did. He said his old man had died and he wanted to stay with his people now.

OAK. And eat what? Fool. He kicked at the food, shelter, clean clothes and free phone that he was getting here. For what? To live a half-clothed, half-starved existence with his people. I tell you. How do we bring development to this lot? (*Peon brings in tea*) So tomorrow's the great day, huh? The big chair. And on 15 August, you will launch the project. The gleaming road. Another iron mine. A new iron-and-steel factory. Three million tonnes of the precious stuff by 2030. That's what you call a future.

THADANI. Long years ago we made a tryst with destiny, (*Everybody grins widely*) and now the time comes when we shall redeem our pledge, in full measure. At the stroke of high noon, when the world is wide awake, we shall hear the ring of your axe against the soft earth in a symbolic act of conquest. Man over Nature. Man for Man. Man for the future.

JEET. It is not a conquest, Mr Thadani. It is accepting with gratitude what Mother Earth offers us with her infinite love and limitless generosity. सुवर्णपुष्पां पृथिवीं चिन्वन्ति पुरूषास्त्रयः | शूरश्च कृतविद्यश्च यश्च जानाति सेवितुम् | The earth gives all her wealth to the chivalrous, the learned and the ones who devote themselves to service.

OAK. Well put. Very well put. Conquest is a word born in Western cultures. For us, the word is love. The most precious gift a mother can give. What a thing a mother is. (*Pause. He looks at the other two. They nod slightly.*) There is a deep sorrow in our hearts which we must express. We are infinitely sad at your mother's passing away. (*Pause*) And your dear friend Karan's tragic death. Tragedies often come together. Your mother was a pativrata. She worshipped her husband, even suffered poverty for his ideas. Your friend was a learned man, the kind of man we value in our society. We cannot understand why he should have chosen the path he did. We believe he died in that terrible fire down in the village?

*Jeet's face is stony, his teeth clenched.*

THADANI. We heard he led the villagers in the satyagraha and died with them. That was a murderous act. Not one that a philosopher-poet should have committed.

PATEL. . . . Not just murderous. Treacherous.

THADANI. But you have borne your sorrows well. A leader must forget personal sorrows in the service of the people.

OAK. The Academy sends you its congratulations. I hope you will visit them soon to take their blessings.

JEET. I have already made plans to do that. Will you excuse me now?

Prince is here to take care of you. Please have more tea.

OAK (*offended*). No, no, no. We are leaving. We are all busy men, after all. (*They rise.*)

PRINCE. A photo, a photo before you go.

*They all stand together: Jeet in the centre, Oak and Thadani on one side and Patel and Prince on the other. Prince holds up a phone on a selfie stick. They smile. The selfie is taken. Everybody laughs. Touching of feet and blessings follow. Thadani, Oak and Patel depart. Prince goes to see them off.*

JEET (*to Peon*). Go feed Raja. I think he's hungry. The first peak is mine. Who would have thought that a boy in flappy pajamas and sadra, who once wrote poetry and had no clue what to do with his life, would rise to these heights. Look, Ma, I am at the top of the see-saw and no one's going to bring me down. I have worked hard. I have thought deeply. I have balanced right against wrong and chosen what is good for our land. And for me. Karan, do you remember Tamburlaine's speech that I recited for one of our competitions? We thought then that Tamburlaine's overweening ambition was wrong. But I will confess now that I thought he was magnificent, pushing himself to work relentlessly, never resting until he possessed the ultimate reward . . .

'That perfect bliss and sole felicity,
The sweet fruition of an earthly crown.'

Imagine, Karan, what a man to have dreamt of an earthly crown.

(*He stands erect and still, then begins to slump. Looks around for something to hold on to. Finding nothing, he sinks to his knees.*)

But, oh, what do I do with this leaden ball that fills my stomach and grows, and grows and grows, till I am faint with fear? Oh, this terrible loneliness. No poetry, no song, no books. No mother, no friend, no beloved. Only foes and flatterers. Where once there was Karan now there is Prince—a hyperion to a satyr. But what's there to fear in being alone? Being alone is my strength.

(*'Maili Chadar' begins softly in Ma's voice. He gets up. Squares his shoulders.*)

When I rise tomorrow, it will be as one of the most powerful men in the country destined for 'that perfect bliss and sole felicity / The sweet fruition of an earthly crown.'

(*Long pause. The song grows louder.*)

Your song doesn't affect me, Ma. Actually, I love it. What is the raag? Khamaj? More like Mishra Khamaj. Right? Like our damned country. Mishra. Everything mixed. I'll straighten it out, you'll see. A single focus. A single colour. A single path. Sing away, I don't care. It's just some musical notes ornamenting a bunch of words as far as I'm concerned. That's what it is. That's ALL that it is. Nothing more (*His voice is rising*)

Absolutely nothing more. It means nothing to me. Nothing.

(*Hands on ears. Shouting*)

NOTHING. So you can stop singing. I said stop singing. Stop. STOP IT, YOU BITCH!

(*Song snaps off. A moment's silence. He removes his hands from his ears. Stands horrified*)

No. No. I didn't mean that, Ma. I didn't. You believe me don't you, Ma? You do. Yes, you do. Thank you, Ma.

(*Raja begins to yap.*)

Are you offended, Raja? Because I said bitch. Should I have said Mrs Dog? (*Laughs*) Sorry my friend. Didn't mean to offend you.

(*Raja continues to yap*)

He is really offended.

*(Jeet begins to laugh as he walks towards the wings.)*

I said sorry, didn't I?

*The dog continues to yap. The man continues to laugh. The barking gets hysterical and so does the laughter. The two sounds merge as Jeet exits.*

## EPILOGUE

PEON (*dressed in his colourful shirt*). Hello, again. You must have missed me. I live in the village now. But I had to come back to end what I had started. Before I go—you'll know by and by where I'm going—I must redeem my word to you. When we first met some 20 years ago, I said our actors were going to present *Maili Chadar, or The Stained Shawl: A Tragedy in Four Acts*. Time to check whether they delivered on the promise. 'Maili Chadar' has been played on the soundtrack a few times and the play was four acts long. That justifies the greater part of the title. The question that remains is why I called it a tragedy. Our hero has not died as he should have in a tragedy. He has, instead, risen to great heights. Other people have died. But those deaths cannot be held as tragic. My great-grandpa died doing his sacred duty, burnt to cinders in the sacred grove. That is a good death. The other villagers: ditto. Karan stood up for his convictions. So his death too was a good death if death can be called good. Ma died of old age and illness. But maybe also of a broken heart. Perhaps her death could be seen as partly tragic. There's nothing more tragic that a mother who sees her son betray all that she and his father stood for. A sadhu died for singing a song. But his life, as Prince pointed out, didn't count. One brave woman is rotting in jail. Is that tragic? In a way, yes. But in a way, no. It is possible that justice will be done as it often is in our country, and she will be free again.

So whose tragedy is it? Mine? I do not have the attributes of the classic tragic hero. I am no Prince of Denmark or Roman general, whose death might make the public weep. As my guru Shakespeare says, 'When beggars die, there are no comets seen; The heavens themselves blaze forth the death of princes.' Anyway, I am not even going to die. I am going to be arrested on false charges. It has been decided I was one of the arsonists who set fire to the two jeeps full of explosives.

What those jeeps were doing near the sacred grove is not a question anybody will ask. And why they were full of explosives will also not be considered of any import. The police have found a man whom they can hold responsible for that terrible fire, and they will soon be here to arrest him. I shall go with them in all docility, because I know in the Great Indian Nation, People Like Me are guilty till they are proved innocent. When the police come for me, you will see what a versatile actor I am. It'll be a relief to display my talents to you after being nothing but a piece of furniture for over two hours. Meanwhile, let me tell you, the iron has entered my soul. In-between the beatings I expect to get in the stinking jail, I shall study the Constitution. For when I come out . . . oh, I certainly will come out, because, most fortunately for us, the law requires indubitable proof of guilt before I can be put away for life. And the police have none. So I shall study the Constitution in order to make it the weapon with which to carry on Great-grandpa's fight. Oh, oh. Sorry, Great-grandpa. My fight.

So is this play a tragedy or isn't it? I think it is. Because when a man without a conscience rules the country, the country is doomed. But you may have a different view. In the few minutes before I am taken away, let me say goodbye to you in the way an Adivasi is expected to. We are supposed to be the simple people, the happy people, people who break into song and dance at the drop of a tourist topi. So here is my song:

This is not goodbye / For I'll soon be back / If not me, another guy
There's many of me / On this teeming earth / If one goes, another comes.
This is not goodbye / I can tell you that / This is not goodbye

*The song continues in the wings, beginning with one voice and then quickly growing to many, like a chant. Peon breaks into a dance which becomes frenzied as the song proceeds: 'This is not goodbye / For he'll soon be back / If not him another guy / There's many of us / On this teeming earth / If one goes, another comes / Stronger and angrier / Than the one before / Watch out then / You men out there / This is not goodbye / This is not goodbye.'*

*Thadani, Oak and Patel enter on cue as policemen. They slap the ground angrily with their canes. Song and dance stop.*

PATEL. Singing eh? And dancing?

OAK. After you've burnt down government property.

THADANI. Sedition. And no shame.

*They slap him.*

PEON (*bawling*). Please, sir, have mercy on a poor man. I didn't do it. (*They slap him a few more times*) Please, sir. Sorry, sir. I did it. I am a sinner. I deserve to die. (*They slap him some more. He is on the ground, pleading. They pull him up and slap him a bit more while he repeats, 'Please, sir, spare a poor man, sir.' Finally, they handcuff him. Peon winks at audience. Stage whisper*) Good acting, no? Deserves applause. Go on, then. Clap.

*He is pushed into the wing. The policemen whack him with their canes. The chant starts again. As Peon's cries fade, the chant gathers strength till it ends on a crescendo of hissing rage: 'This is not goodbye / This is not goodbye/ He'll be back / This is not goodbye / THIS . . . IS . . . NOT . . . GOODBYE.*

CURTAIN

# TRUTH AND JUSTICE

*Four Monologues*

## Paris, January 1945

### The Cleaning Woman

You can say I started it all. My name has not been recorded in the story although I do have a name like everybody else. But history can't be bothered with the likes of me. Anyway, I must humbly submit that the part I played in the scandal, which people now call the Dreyfus Affair, was very small. At the same time, it must be said that had I not done my bit, the affair wouldn't have unfolded the way it did. Mind you, I am not claiming more credit than I deserve. I was only doing my duty as a patriot.

I remember the day I was honoured to be called into the office of the Section Statistique of the French army. It was on the 22nd of December 1894. I was so proud, so proud to be in such a grand building. Every wall covered with photographs of great men, brave men, men who had fought for the country. High ceilings. Heavy chairs. Carved.

I was led into a big chamber and asked to wait. Me, an ordinary charwoman. Who would have thought it? I sat down, but on the edge, ready to spring up the moment they wanted me to be gone. I wonder why I said 'they'. It was just one man. But what a man. Tall. Moustache. Gold epaulettes. That's something. That's equal to ten ordinary men, train drivers, bartenders, plumbers. He leant across the big table and said, 'Mrs . . . ?'

I muttered my name. He did not hear it. But he said it didn't matter. 'You are, I believe a cleaning woman,' he said, very polite and all. Posh accent.

It was not something I needed to be ashamed of. A cleaning job is a good job. Better than some jobs, like . . . well . . . some jobs. So I said with my head up, 'Yes, I'm a cleaning woman.'

He said, 'Good. And I believe you clean the offices at the German Embassy.'

'I do,' I replied.

'Which includes the office of the military attaché, Lieutenant Colonel Maximilian von Schwartzkoppen?'

'I don't know sir,' I said, a little confused. The embassy is big. There are two more charwomen, one per floor. One whole floor is a whole day's work to keep clean. I rush into each room looking only at the dirt on the floor and the dust on the furniture. I've never seen the names on the doors or anything else. So I said—because why lie?—'I don't know, sir.'

He said, 'That is OK. We know you do. It is the biggest room at the end of the corridor. Next time you enter it, will you please look at the name on the door and report back to me? Do it tomorrow, please. It is rather urgent.'

He said 'please' twice. 'S'il vous plait'! I had to keep this visit a secret from my husband. He would have blown his top to know that a man with gold on his shoulders had asked me, a woman, to do something for him. The next day, I looked at the door of the last room in the corridor and it did say Lieutenant Colonel Maximilian von Schwartzkoppen.

I went back to the grand building where the man with the gold on his shoulders sat and told him, 'Yes, I do clean the room of the gentleman you referred to.'

'I believe you empty the waste paper baskets in the rooms you clean. Is that right?'

'That is right, sir,' I said.

'Well, then. There is a little job I would like you to do for our country. Don't forget, you are the backbone of France. Without people like you, France would be at the bottom of the sea. What you can do for your country is to put the contents of the Lieutenant Colonel's wastepaper basket into a bag and bring it to me every day. Would you do that?'

I didn't know what to say. As it is, I'm late going home every day. Then there is dinner to cook for a hungry family. To come all the way here would . . .

The gentleman saw I was hesitating. He smiled and said, 'We will pay you for your work.'

I was very embarrassed. To think that he thought I wanted money to save France from sinking to the bottom of the sea! I said to him quickly, 'It isn't the money, sir. It is cooking dinner.'

'Oh, that? That is not a problem. We will send you a carriage to save you time. Une petite chaise, madame.'

I was too shocked to speak. I had never stepped into a chaise before. It was a grand thing. But why not, I thought to myself. Why not?

And so I started doing this small job to stop France from sinking to the bottom of the sea.

And that was all there was to it. I have no idea what they did with the waste paper. But then a big scandal broke out, and I heard from here and there that they had discovered a slip of paper from a wastepaper basket in the German Embassy that told the man with gold on his shoulders that somebody in the French army was doing something to plunge France to the bottom of the sea. I was that angry. That angry, I tell you. Here I was trying to keep France afloat, and some devil was dragging it down. But my work paid off. The devil was soon caught and packed off to jail for life.

I was there next January, outside the courtyard of the École Militaire, on the Champ-de-Mars. Emile, my husband, and my little son Francois were with me. There he was, the devil. And I can tell you, I was not a bit surprised when Emile whispered in my ear, 'They say he is a Jewish pig.' Those people are born devils. The army put up a magnificent show. Our soldiers were there, brave men ready to give their lives for France. And here was this devil of a Jew . . . who knows what he had done. But that slip from my bag of waste paper had exposed him. I can't tell you how proud I was that day. I smiled to myself, thinking Emile had no clue that I was behind the dirty Jew's comeuppance.

I looked hard at the man. The devilish thing was he didn't look like the devil. A very ordinary face. A rather stupid face, I'd say. Flat. No expression. But that's how it is with Satan. He pretends he's an ordinary man like your brother or husband. But his heart is evil.

The show started. A soldier took the Jew by the scruff of the neck and pulled off all his stripes, one by one. Then he ripped his army jacket. Then he dragged him around the grounds for us to take a good look at. The soldier called him traitor. But the devil called back in an oh-so-innocent-voice, 'It was not I who wrote that slip. I would never do such a thing. Why are you doing this to me? I love France.'

That got us really angry. Love France indeed! Did he even have the right to utter those sacred words? We spat on him. Called him dirty Jew and Judas. It was the kind of show that we had only heard of till then. In the good old days, so they say, heretics were burnt at the stake and people gathered to watch the fun. It was fun, yes. But it was also a lesson for those spectators. Don't speak against the Church if you want to stay alive.

The show soon ended. It was January and bitterly cold. We were shivering and blue. But back home there was meat boiling in the pot and fresh baked bread. It was a good meal for a winter morning.

It was the middle of October. I got up that morning with a chill in my stomach. My insides had turned to icy bile that swirled around in my gut and rose to my throat, turning my mouth bitter.

The previous morning, they had called Alfred away. The summons was most unexpected. It had never happened before in all the five years of our marriage. Alfred was only a Captain in the French General Staff, a position of no importance. But the message said, 'Report to headquarters at nine in the morning in civilian clothes for an examination of the trainee officers.'

Trainee officers? I asked him. What have you to do with them? Alfred shrugged. He did not know. He could not even guess. But he was the last person to question orders. Little Pierre said, 'I'm coming, Papa.' Alfred said, 'No, you are not.' Pierre said mischievously, 'You didn't let me finish my sentence. I'm coming to the door.'

'You rascal,' Alfred said as he stepped out, laughing. It was a pleasant morning. I recall it distinctly. A puff of breeze blew a deep russet leaf off the horse-chestnut tree before our house. Alfred bent to pick it up and presented it to Pierre. 'See you in the evening,' he said, ruffling Pierre's hair.

And he left.

We didn't see him in the evening.

I waited dinner. It went cold. He didn't come. I didn't eat. I put Pierre and Jeanne to bed. I made up our bed. I waited. He didn't come. I didn't sleep. The next morning, as soon as the nanny arrived, I left, with that icy bile filling my mouth. Where was Alfred? I had to find out. I went to the military headquarters. I told them Alfred had not come home after examining the trainee officers.

The men behind every door I knocked on looked blank. They asked me impatiently, 'Who is Alfred?' and 'What trainee officers?'

It occurred to me that I was asking the wrong people. I should go to the General Staff office where he worked. They would know.

In the General Staff office, I was sent from one chamber to another. Finally, a stern-looking captain told me that Alfred had been charged with treason and arrested. I collapsed in the nearest chair. It was all I could do to drag myself up and go home. I wept all the way till I thought my heart would break.

They brought Alfred to trial in December. He was accused of leaking military secrets to the Germans. I had to laugh. I did laugh. I laughed like a crazy woman while my heart bled.

Our lawyer, Edgar Demange, asked for a public trial. The army held it *in camera*. Lies need the protection of secrecy. Everything was done secretly. A secret dossier was given to the judges in a sealed cover. What did the dossier say? Nobody knew. Although its contents were used to condemn my innocent, loyal, dedicated husband, he didn't know what the dossier contained. Demange didn't know what it contained. I and the world at large were never to know what it contained. The dossier was destroyed after Alfred was convicted. The French army, which was a second home to him, which had given his life meaning, that French Army had turned deliberately deaf to his voice pleading innocence.

(*Edgar Demange's recorded voice*)

*Madame, I did my best. I put all my knowledge, logic, reason, my skills of argument and persuasion at the service of your husband. But to no avail. The only evidence they had was a slip of paper on which the writer had promised to part with military secrets. I argued that the handwriting was not Captain Alfred Dreyfus'. Ask him to write just three words, his name, and compare them to your slip of paper. You will instantly see he did not write it. But madame, justice is blind in many ways. Sometimes it cannot see what is plain to see. Sometimes the blindness is wilful. I do believe justice had turned wilfully blind in your husband's case. Some quack graphologist had already convinced the judges with the most convoluted logic, that the incriminating slip had indeed been written by Alfred Dreyfus. The very lack of resemblance between Dreyfus' writing and that on the slip was proof of 'self-forgery', something that even an amateur crook would do to prevent detection. For which crook would betray himself by using his own handwriting on slips that would incriminate him if they were found?*

*Madame, today I confess to being ashamed of my profession. Even before the trial began, your husband had been convicted for treason.*

Alfred was convicted and sentenced to life imprisonment. What does life imprisonment mean for a family man of 35, father of two young children? His last words to his son were, 'See you in the evening.' That evening was going to be the evening of his life. What does a woman who loves her husband passionately do with such knowledge? Every day she cooks, she washes, she cleans and dies in her heart.

When Alfred was on trial, I went to see him in prison. I found a man broken in body and spirit. Within a few days he had shrunk. Everything about him was pinched. He had asked for a revolver. He had given up hope. Seeing him like that put life back into me. I held his hand, I told him there was hope. We were going to appeal. His dear brother Mathieu was spending every waking minute gathering more evidence to prove his innocence. Demange was putting the new evidence together for the appeal. The evidence pointed the finger at another man altogether. The real traitor.

Eight days later, Alfred's appeal was rejected. The new evidence was barely considered. They had their man and they were not going to let him go. Alfred was informed that he would undergo the ritual of military degradation before being sent to prison to serve his sentence.

The memory of that January morning still brings back, these four decades later, when Alfred has been dead and buried ten years, the rage that consumed me then. Like an inferno bursting out of every pore of my skin, ready to burn the world of men to cinders. Men know how to humiliate men. Rituals are devised as spectacles to assure citizens that they and the nation are safe. But men enjoy what they do. I was looking at the soldier chosen to humiliate Alfred in the courtyard of the École Militaire. I saw the devilish joy on his face. I wanted to claw at it, gouge out those gleaming eyes. But I reined in my rage. The spectacle was going to help me understand the human race. There were two kinds of men before me: there was Alfred who stood erect as his stripes were torn off, one by one, his proud military jacket ripped, and his sword, the weapon he had carried with such pride, broken by the soldier over his knees. And there was the soldier who had once marched shoulder to shoulder with Alfred, doing his duty by the nation.

But he was only acting the part. The spectacle was as false as the charge of treason. A tailor had visited Alfred's cell the previous evening, taken off his stripes and put them back on with a single stitch. A sword-maker had visited his cell after the tailor, broken his sword in two and put it together again with a weak joint. The soldier who ripped off the stripes and broke the sword with such vengeful glee was only pretending to put all his strength into it. Falsehood upon falsehood upon falsehood, all to trap and humiliate a truthful man. The irony of it!

And what did Alfred say as he was paraded around the ground? 'You are degrading an innocent man! Long live France! Long live the army!' As he passed the crowds gathered to watch his humiliation, he shouted again, 'Long live France! Long live the army.' The crowd shouted back 'Jew!' 'Judas!'

(*The curtain at the back parts to reveal a picture.*)

This illustration appeared in *Le Petit Journal* whose editor was the leader of France's Jew-haters. I must give him some credit, though, for showing Alfred standing erect and stoic. Surely a Jew and a Judas should have been depicted as a craven creature with a crooked spine?

(*She looks at the picture for a few seconds. The curtain closes*)

'Truth will out' is a cliche. It suggests an ultimate triumph that comes as a reward for the pain you have suffered. But there is little triumph when the truth is preceded by so much untruth and so many years of torture. The scars those experiences leave are permanent. The revelation of truth then is an abstract thing. Oh yes, the truth was out, but the man I had known before was not the man who came back to me five years later. Where was he then? Devoured by a gigantic untruth, deliberately created and deliberately executed. But they had not managed to warp Alfred's essence. His love for his family was intact, his faith in himself and his country was intact. He was ready to resume life where he had left off. We lived a happy life, he into his seventies and I till now.

I often wonder what kind of man Alfred was. He did not carry even a shred of resentment against those who had taken away five years of his prime and been niggardly even in the justice they were finally forced to grant. The years of torture and humiliation are all here, captured in this report.

(*She picks a sheet off a pile that lies on the stool next to her. She reads*)

'Dreyfus was transported to Devil's Island like a low wretch. Besides his guard, he was the only inhabitant of that godforsaken island. A stone hut 13 x 13 feet had been specially built for him. It was dank and dark, overrun by mice and other vermin. Temperatures on the island sometimes reached 50 degrees. Although his prison was on an island, he was not allowed a single glimpse of the sea, so haunted were his keepers at the thought of his escape. He fell sick and was shaken by fevers which grew worse by the day. He was given scraps to eat as food. He lost his voice.'

(*She looks up, her face blank with misery*)

When he returned, he could only speak in a hoarse whisper. Devil's Island. How apt the name was. Nobody had heard of it. It lay off the coast of French Guiana, all the way across the Atlantic. They had made sure I could not even think of visiting him. I used to visit when he was in prison here, during his trial. I visited him even in the prison where he was sent while the farce of his appeal was played out. But why allow a traitor, a Jew to boot, the comfort of a wife's visits when you can put him in a hole away from all humanity? He deserved the place because he was twice guilty. He was a traitor. But also one who refused to accept his guilt.

When he was convicted, he was given the opportunity to choose the only 'honorable way out'. A loaded revolver was placed in his cell. How easy life would have been for his judges had he pulled the trigger on himself. But Alfred would do no such a thing. He wanted to live, for himself, for his family, for France. He wanted to prove, against all odds, that he was innocent.

On the day he was convicted and sentenced, he received a visit from the man who had dictated the accusation of treason committed by Captain Alfred Dreyfus to Captain Alfred Dreyfus himself. Alfred had been made to write his own chargesheet. And this man, Du Paty de Clam, had now been sent by the Minister of War to tell Alfred that he might obtain a mitigation of the sentence if he made a confession and revealed the nature of his misdeeds. Alfred said, 'I have nothing to confess.' He asked only that the investigation be continued so that the real criminal was finally discovered and punished. Even as they dragged him away and loaded him on to the *Ville de St. Nazaire* like an animal being sent to slaughter, he was saying, 'I am going but let them keep searching for the real culprit. It is the only favour I ask'. When he reached his destination after a rough 15-day voyage, he was horrified at what he saw.

(*Reads from another sheet*)

'They could not have sent me to a more godforsaken place. I had been told by my prison guards back in France that I was being given the worst punishment possible for not having confessed to my guilt.'

(*She looks up. Angrily*)

His predetermined guilt. Fixed before they even saw his face. He had nothing to do with the act he was accused of. Meanwhile, the man who had everything to do with it was roaming free. Major Ferdinand Walsin Esterhazy. That was his name. One of the many Dreyfussards who had fought hard for Alfred's acquittal put it rather neatly in his letter to me.

(*Draws another sheet from the pile and reads*)

'Esterhazy had done everything short of wearing a nametag on his shirtfront reading "Spy". I am not one to hold a man's lineage against him in judging his actions. But in this case the two matched so perfectly that I must mention that his mother was an illegitimate daughter of an illegitimate claimant to the Hungarian royal line. He had often spoken of his hatred for the French army. He was notorious in the Army for being a drunk and in perpetual debt. How is it that nobody, not a single one of those powerful men decorated with gold, wondered whether Esterhazy might not be a likelier man to have sold secrets to the Germans than a Jewish family man?'

(*She puts the sheet back. Looks up with empty eyes.*)

Why did they not wonder? The thought returns to me again and again, although Alfred tried hard to dislodge it from my mind. They did not wonder because Alfred was a Jew. He was guilty at birth. Whether or not he had committed the crime he was charged with was a matter of mere detail. A Jew deserved the most brutal punishment possible for being what he was. Alfred never did believe his punishment had anything to do with his being a Jew. Because in his rotten prison, he could not hear the anti-Semitic dogs of France baying for his blood, gloating, cheering at what had been done to him. In my more charitable moments I am willing to concede that perhaps anti-Semitism didn't start the Dreyfus Affair. But anybody who was in France during those years could see as plain as the noses on their faces that anti-Semitism fuelled it.

As though Alfred's suffering in his dank, dark hovel wasn't enough, a newspaper falsely reported on 3 September 1896 that he had made an attempt to escape. How? Did he break through all the barriers that held him? Did he then catch his guard napping? Did he jump into the Atlantic Ocean in an attempt to reach America?

The Jew-haters of Paris added other false reports. The prison administration was put on full alert. The colonial secretary, André Lebon, took fright. It did not matter that he knew these tales to be unfounded, that he knew the prisoner to be of irreproachable conduct. Lebon wanted to make doubly sure that he stayed that way. He cabled instructions to the governor of Guiana to surround the outer boundary of Alfred's exercising-ground with a solid fence. Until the work was finished, he was to be shackled day and night to his bed by means of the dreaded 'double buckle'. For 24 days and nights, he lay flat on his back, unable to move. Even when the shackles were removed, he was not allowed to stir out of his filthy, vermin-ridden hut. When he finally did, he found a 6-foot-high wall around him which cut off even the tiniest glimpse of sea and sky. All he had now to walk in was a narrow passage between the hut and the wall.

This is what they did to my gentle, honest, beloved, upright Alfred.

(*Weeps*)

I got to know these details only later. His letters to me and mine to him were opened and read, and only those parts which his jailers decided would do no harm, were copied and sent on. What enraged me was that while Alfred was given only a strip of ground to walk in, Esterhazy was roaming free. Finally, public pressure forced the army to try him. But, as anybody would have guessed, he was acquitted. You don't believe it? Then you don't know the hubris that drives men in power. It takes moral strength to admit you have done a grave injustice to an innocent man. It takes only hubris to continue with the injustice. Let the real traitor walk and to hell with the welfare of the nation and its people.

Esterhazy's acquittal so horrified Emile Zola that he wrote an open letter to the President of France. It was titled 'J'Accuse' and published in *L'Aurore*. It ridiculed the law of the country for having let off the real traitor while keeping an innocent man illegally imprisoned. Zola was tried, convicted and sentenced to a year in prison for having had the gumption to address the President and to deride French justice, all in the interests of that piffling thing called truth. How angry it makes me even today, as I stand before you, to think that a bunch of arrogant men should have had the power to turn falsehood into truth and truth into falsehood. Was God even looking?

Poor Zola. He exiled himself to England to escape imprisonment. The revelations he had made in 'J'Accuse', followed by his trial and conviction shocked England. Shocked America. But France remained unmoved. Zola wrote an open letter to me too in *L'Aurore* when the case against Alfred was finally reopened.

(*She picks up a sheet from the pile and reads*)

'We have been promised, in compensation, the justice of history. For me, I hope that the revenge of history will be more serious than the delights of paradise. A little justice on this earth would have pleased me . . . and I'm still waiting.'

The great writer did not live to see justice done. It was finally, but four years after he died of asphyxiation. So hated was he for his views that one of his many enemies blocked his chimney. Zola inhaled the fumes and died. Another such enemy shot at Alfred when he attended Zola's funeral.

Enough of this. Enough. These things happened 40 years ago. And yet, when I speak of them today, I still want to scream and cry and kill. I often ask myself why I cannot forgive. Alfred forgave although he spent 1,517 days on Devil's Island, from 13 April 1895 to 9 June 1899. All that time, he kept his spirits up by reading, writing a diary, returning to his old love, mathematics, learning English, striving to save his body from crumbling and his brain from rotting. And me? For 40 years I have held on to my bitterness and I am not sorry for it.

On 26 December 1898, when there was hope that Alfred's name would be cleared, he wrote to me.

(*She reads from a sheet.*)

'When one has lived a life of duty, of complete honour, when one has known only one single language, the language of Truth, it is a source of strength, I assure you, and no matter how horrible fate may be, one must be noble-minded enough to overcome it and to make it bow down before you.'

That was my Alfred, a simple, trusting, honest and loyal man. And then there are those in this world who will kill out of sheer hatred and declare it is for their God and country. How can any killing be for God who loves all living creatures, the two-legged, the four legged, the furred and the feathered? How can any killing be for the country when your own are killed along with those whom you deem the enemy?

Alfred's retrial was as much of a farce as his trial. Despite all the evidence that Mathieu had gathered to prove his innocence, he was convicted again. But this time his 10-year sentence was qualified with a reference to 'extenuating circumstances'. This meant that, although the Army couldn't be seen to overturn its own verdict, it was admitting it had been wrong. As compensation, they offered Alfred an amnesty which would set him free on condition that he not protest his innocence. Dear Mathieu, who had worked so hard on his beloved brother's behalf, bowed to the intolerable condition for Alfred's freedom. The Dreyfussards were profoundly upset. They had not risked their reputations and lives for such half measures. They wanted to go to appeal yet again. So indeed did I. Alfred himself wasn't sure what should be done. But Mathieu was more clear-headed than any of us. He persuaded us that the amnesty was as close to an admission of wrongdoing as we could hope to get from the French army and politicians.

Yes, politicians. Politics had had much to do with the result of Alfred's appeal. The half-hearted acquittal he was given was not entirely because the army had suddenly discovered its error. It was because of political and economic expediency. You may remember that 1900 was the year of the Paris Exposition. The Zola trial had awakened the consciences of some powerful people in France and around the world. The Exposition was going to put France's prestige and the capital's income on the line. The great fear was that if they continued to persecute Alfred, many foreign powers would stay away from the Exposition. Some countries had already indicated they would.

Another four years had to pass before Alfred was fully exonerated. He was re-instated in his beloved army in 1906, promoted and even awarded the Legion d'Honneur. He accepted the honour with grace because that was Alfred. I found it more difficult to do so. I searched my soul again to discover why. Why could I not forgive as easily as he? Perhaps because forgiveness had not been asked for. Nobody had said sorry. Nobody had shown a shred of remorse. Weren't these men human beings? Did they not for a moment feel that they had put a good, honest, innocent man through years of torture on a trumped-up charge? Did they not ask themselves why he had been unable to serve in his beloved French army for more than a year after his re-instatement. He wasn't old. He was only 46. But they had destroyed his body. The body that had been so brutally tortured on Devil's Island could not take the stress of army life.

I have reached the age of 74. That is old. But I feel even older. We are still in the middle of the Second World War. I volunteered during the First in the hope that, when it ended, men would have learnt the futility of war with its tragic toll of lives. That they would have grown to understand the value of love over anger and hatred, of compassion and tolerance over power. I wish I had not lived to see that men do not learn from history. One of these days, I'll be gone. I will not regret it. I now know that men will continue to shed blood in defence of God and country.

Ecce homo. Behold the man. Alfred on the one hand, Esterhazy on the other. I hate to say it but I must, because that is what my 74 years on earth have taught me: the Esterhazys of this world will always get away. The Alfreds of this world will always suffer.

**Byculla, 2006**

*A prison cell. A young girl sits on the floor with her back to the wall, hugging her knees to her chest. This is Zaheera Sheikh.*

For the first time in 12 months I feel safe. These bars imprison me. But they also keep the world out.

(*Pause*)

Are there others like me, 16, 17, 18-year-olds, who have come to fear the world?

(*She stands up and stretches.*)

It's a small cell. But this is room enough for me. I don't care if I don't see the sky. I don't care if I don't feel the breeze on my skin. I don't care if I don't hear the song of birds. I care that I have the freedom to simply be. To remember. To think. To ask myself what happened. What brought me here. To sift through my experiences and see what I am left with.

I am here for a year. This year may not pass as swiftly as some years have done in my life, years of laughter, family, eating and playing. But it will pass soon enough, and I must have my answers ready by then. Because then I will step out of this safe haven to face the world again. I will be free.

(*Smiles wryly*)

Free to run. To hide. They are out there, the men who hounded me, harassed me, threatened me till I was forced to tell the fatal untruth that I shall forever be ashamed of.

I don't ever want to meet those men again. But they are my world. They live where I live. I have nowhere else to go. I will have to face them. I know I will have my guardian's support. But from outside. I will need something that will support me from inside . . . I don't know what to call it . . . Spirit? Spine? Something that will give me the strength to insist on living even though they want me dead. I know one thing: I am a better human being than them. I have never intentionally hurt anyone. Will that thought hold me together?

I need not feel ashamed before them of what I did. They have done much worse. They have done things that are a blot on Allah's world. I will hold my head up before them. But when I am alone, my conscience will trouble me. It troubles me here. It won't let me sleep. I hear voices. Abbu's, Chachu's, my little sister's. And then I hear my guardian's voice telling the newspaper man how brave I was, how truthful. I had told the police all I had seen, exactly as it happened. Without fear.

It seems so long ago now . . . those years when I was innocent enough not to know fear. My guardian was old enough to see the future even then. He knew we would always have to live in fear. He asked the newspaper man not to publish his name. He had been so proud of his name. Now he wanted to hide it. Can men do worse than make an honest, hard-working man want to hide his name?

When I was thrown into the world of those men, that is when I too knew fear.

Is fearing for your life not reason enough to lie?

(*Long pause.*)

So I lied.

(*She paces the floor. Turns and speaks*)

YES. I LIED UNDER OATH. But who in that court of law didn't? Name one man or woman who didn't. They all lied—the murderers' lawyer who put words into my mouth. My lawyer who allowed him to do that. My own Ammi who always told me that Allah hates liars.

My brother, the only male member of the family left alive. Every single person in that court, the place that is supposed to be the home of truth and justice, lied. Yet, only I have been punished. The guilty have been acquitted of their horrendous crimes.

Poor Abbu. When I think of him, I weep.

(*She bangs her head against the wall.*)

How hard he worked to feed and clothe us. What was he? A poor man from Uttar Pradesh, looking to make a decent living. He had heard of Vadodara as a fine city, cultured, prosperous. He thought he could make a good life there. And he did too. As good a life as an illiterate, unskilled man can. He found a job in a bakery. He learnt the ropes. Scrimped and saved to buy his own place. He named it Best Bakery. He was so proud of the name. It was English. It declared his bakery was the best. He was proud of the bread we made. Oh, the fragrance of it!

(*She sniffs the air and smiles*)

Yes. We did make the best bread. We fed our neighbours the best bread they had ever had. They swore by our bread. They lived on our bread. But when the time came, they shut their doors against us, while we, the makers of their bread, were burnt alive.

(*Long pause. Her face is filled with pain as she relives the horror of that day.*)

They weren't just neighbours. They were also friends. But I cannot blame them. They too had seen the murderous faces of the mob. A mob is a terrifying beast. Those who have never faced a mob will never know the fear that a mob puts into you. You have seen those men individually with their wives, their children. You have seen them eat and drink. You have celebrated festivals with them. Then they come together, armed, and become this mass of limbs and eyes with a single heart, full of anger and hatred.

(*She paces the floor again. Comes to a halt.*)

Was I responsible for that mob? Had I, Zaheera Sheikh, done something in my 16 years to turn its monstrous heart against me? Is that why they decided Zaheera Sheikh's family must be burnt alive? She needs to be taught a lesson? Zaheera means shining, luminous. Were they offended by my name? Did they decide that the only way to punish me for daring to shine was to turn my life into one long hopeless night, without moon or stars?

I doubt if they would have answers to my questions. I doubt they think I even deserve answers. So what do you have? A mindless heartless mob. And what are you to it? A mere nothing. They are many. You are alone. Your only thought is to save yourself.

(*She looks up at the ceiling, then straight ahead.*)

When the mob came, some of us ran to the terrace. Some locked themselves on the first floor. The flames leapt up. They licked at the ground floor. Devoured it. They rose higher. To the first floor. The floor of the terrace grew so hot, we had to dance from foot to foot to keep our soles from being roasted. The flames enveloped us and shot up into the sky. We ran to the front where the floor was still holding up. The flames lit up the faces of the men down below. I recognized every one of them, their ghoulish faces lit orange and red. I named them all to the police and to the newspapers. I rattled off 21 names.

(*She stands up straight, face front, chin raised, back erect.*)

I TOLD THE TRUTH. It went into the police files, into newspaper reports. Those 21 men knew they had been named. I was catapulted into the public eye. I was the star witness in the Best Bakery case. I did not know it then . . . I was only 16 . . . that there is a price you pay for telling the truth. Surely those august men of law in their black coats knew it? Surely the police knew it? Surely the newspaper editors knew it? How is it that none of these great, knowledgeable men, failed to warn me of the dangers of truth? Why did they not think I would have to be protected from those 21 men if I was to continue speaking the truth?

(*She sighs and smiles crookedly.*)

More questions without answers. The fact remains: I was not warned. I was not protected. Perhaps because nobody cared about the truth. Perhaps because nobody cared about me. Who was I, after all? Hundreds had been murdered. One more would make no difference.

(*She pulls herself up*)

But it made a difference to me. I was nothing to them. But I was something to me. I had a very simple wish. Ants have it. Snails have it. Crows have it. I wanted to live. But I also wanted to tell the world what I had seen those 21 men do. The first time I was in court, I did stand up and tell the truth—the same truth I had told the police and the newspapers. 'The mob came. They burnt our place down. The men and women who died in that fire were my family and bakery employees. My father ran out, trying to save himself. They pushed him back in.' I rattled off the names of the men who had done it. I pointed them out to the court. I don't know where I found the courage to do that. Because when I stood up, I looked around the crowded court to see if I could spot a friendly face. There was none. I did not see a single Muslim face, neither friend, family nor neighbour. Not even a member of the committee that had been formed to help victims of the massacre like us. Despite that, I told the truth. And then?

(*She shudders at the memory.*)

Then I stepped out of the court. I was alone. No family. No lawyer. Instead, walking towards me were two of the men I had named. They said: we will drop you home in our car, and hustled me into it.

Did nobody see them do that? The police? They were there in huge numbers, chests out, canes swinging. Did they step forward and say to the men: she is our witness, we will take her home? Did my lawyer step forward to take my arm and lead me to safety? No. And no. And no. The murderers hustled me into their car, and I found myself sitting between two killers. They said only one thing to me. 'This is the last time you will tell the lies you told today in court. If you do it again, we'll burn you alive too. *Tamne pan jeevta salagavi deshe.*'

Would I not believe the threat? I had seen them murder. They were not human. And I was a rag doll, of no use to anybody. Who out there can say, after a threat like that from men like them, that they would not have lied? Even under oath?

(*She lowers her head for a moment. Then looks up.*)

I never did tell the truth again. I had been a star witness, my picture had been plastered everywhere. Now I was the villain. When my picture is published now, it is always with a caption that I had done another flip-flop. Once I was branded as a villain, other questions began to be asked. Reporters went about with spy cameras, listening in on conversations the murderers were having. The murderers were saying they had paid me 18 lakhs to lie. A poor girl with no family left is offered 18 lakhs. She once had a home. Now it is a charred shell. She has tried to sell it. But the neighbours have spread a rumour. The place is haunted. Who would want to buy a haunted house? I could not sell it. It remains a shell. It will soon pass into the murderers' hands for free.

Why did my neighbours whose children I had grown up playing with, spread such rumours? Because they were no longer neighbours and friends. They were Hindu and I was Muslim. We were no longer human beings. We were not even Indians. We were either Hindu. Or Muslim.

The committee set up to help us rebuild our lives had built houses for us. But we had to pay 50,000 rupees if we wanted one of them. I didn't have a single rupee that I could call my own. My kind, honest guardian pleaded with the committee. Give her a roof, he said. She will pay you 50,000 in time. I will help her pay it. She is a brave girl. She is a hard-working girl. She is young and strong. She will find work. But she needs your help now.

Did they listen to him? No. Rules are rules. Pay 50,000 and here's your roof.

The future had closed its doors on me. Then I was allegedly offered 18 lakhs, a sum I had not seen even in my dreams. If I had been offered the money, I would have seen a future before me. I would have taken it. My guardian would have been unhappy. But he would have understood. He would have prayed to Allah to forgive me. But was the money given to me? Go find out, you reporters. Where's your proof that the money came to me? But you have proof of those murderers saying they gave it to me. Does that not damn them? The court needs to ask them a few questions. Why had they offered to pay me that money? The court needs to say, 'If you paid her money, it is proof that you wanted to suppress the truth. You did not want her to tell the truth in court. That makes you guilty. YOU ARE GUILTY, DAMN YOU. GUILTY.'

(*She slides to the floor and leans against the wall.*)

Fear of death, hope for the future, whatever the reason for the lies I told, I can't say my conscience is clear. How can it be? I have betrayed my family. But I have learnt an important truth about human beings. There are ordinary human beings and there are heroic human beings. I remember reading the story of a French girl called Joan who was burnt at the stake. She was almost the same age as me when she died. But she was not afraid. Nothing, no bribes, no threats stopped her from telling the truth.

I am not Joan. I am neither hero nor saint. I am an ordinary girl who wants to live. When I am out of here, I shall keep my mouth shut. Those 21 men have been set free by a law that is supposed to stand for truth and justice. I know it does nothing of the kind. The law didn't care for truth enough to allow me to continue speaking it without fear. I say here and now that the gravest injustice has been done to me. The court is not a home of truth and justice. I am not guilty before it. I am guilty only before my father, my uncle, my sister. And Allah.

But Allah is merciful. He will forgive me. Meanwhile I will live. That is all I want. I want to live.

## THE YOUNG JOURNALIST'S MONOLOGUE

**Mumbai, 2021**

My name is S. Let's leave it at that. It embarrasses me to spell it out. I am 30, but I still haven't lived up to it. It's a tough call to live up to such a name, particularly today. And the profession I belong to makes it almost impossible. My profession has forgotten to walk upright. When our top men bend, they force people down the line to bend with them. We flunkeys have no choice. Don't say this, don't mention him, go easy here, why do you want to investigate that? What's your problem? You don't like the way things are? There's the door.

I think wistfully of the pictures that illustrate Darwinian evolution. The last picture shows Man walking upright, looking bravely at the world. My profession has lost both abilities: to walk upright, and to look bravely at the world.

We were taught the history of my profession at journalism school. We were once called the Fourth Estate. We served as an agency of public discussion. We offered a platform to rival ideas and interests. They competed with each other until the truth prevailed. Nobody calls us the Fourth Estate any longer. Nobody even calls us a pillar of democracy. The Estate is lost. The pillar has collapsed. We are now a product, like toothpaste, looking for as large a market as we can capture.

I have been part of this profession for seven years. Every day, I have struggled to feel proud of what I am doing. I am about to give up. I want to quit. Opt out. Escape. I have a good MBA degree. I can get a job that is many times more lucrative than this. If I must prostitute myself, let me do it for more money. Why solicit on the streets when I can be a concubine to kings?

Lasantha Wickrematunge, I owe you an apology. You have been my ideal, my inspiration. The reason why I'm here. You did not quit. You stuck it out. Today is 8 January 2021. On this day, 12 years ago, you were assassinated. You had predicted your death. You wrote an article and told your readers why you had invited death upon yourself. You wanted your newspaper to publish it posthumously. They did, three days after you were shot down by unknown assailants. The assailants were unknown. Yes. But you knew on whose orders they had done it. On the orders of Sri Lankan President. Mahinda Rajapaksa.

The class was shocked into silence when that article was forwarded to us and we were invited to respond. Some of us were in tears. Some said, you were right. Others said the president was right. A country cannot afford to let anti-nationals roam free. You are surprised? You wouldn't be if you were alive today. Patriotism and nationalism are sacred words, defined by how many acts of violence you commit against the enemy. The enemy is predetermined. Nobody questions that. As children, we sorted out our fights with the line, 'Majority wins'. That was democracy. That is democracy now. Majority wins. Minority, whether by race, religion or ideas, is the enemy.

You did not think so. You refused to side with the majority.

During the class discussion, some people quoted a passage from your article and said you belonged to an older generation. They pointed out that you had died twelve years ago. Twelve years is a long time in a rapidly developing world where new technologies have given voice to people who had no voice in your time. Ideas like yours wouldn't work today they said. What ideas were they referring to?

(*She opens her laptop and reads.*)

'Our commitment is to see Sri Lanka as a transparent, secular, liberal democracy. Think about those words, for each has a profound meaning.

Transparent, because government must be openly accountable to the people and never abuse their trust. Secular, because in a multi-ethnic and multi-cultural society such as ours, secularism offers the only common ground by which we might all be united. Liberal, because we recognize that all human beings are created different, and we need to accept others for what they are and not what we would like them to be. And democratic . . . well, if you need me to explain why that is important, you'd best stop buying this paper.'

My MBA friends stood solidly against me when I told them of my admiration for you. They said a nation needs a strong leader. Rajapaksa was one such. I said a nation needs a wise, compassionate leader who will take everybody with him, not divide people with inflammatory speeches and violent acts. They said you were silly to give up your life for old-fashioned ideas. You would have done more good by staying alive. Life is about subterfuge and strategy, they said, not idiotic heroism. I was angry. I said: what about all those young people like us who died for our freedom? Were they silly? What about the people of Myanmar who think nothing of facing a brutal junta's bullets? Why do they do it? Are they silly? No. They are fighting for democracy. How can you dismiss democracy as an old-fashioned idea?

You too had friends like mine.

(*Reads*)

'No other profession calls on its practitioners to lay down their lives for their art save the armed forces. And in Sri Lanka, journalism. Why then do we do it? After all, I too am a husband, and father of three wonderful children. I too have responsibilities and obligations that transcend my profession, be it the law or journalism. Is it worth the risk? Many people tell me it is not. Friends tell me to revert to the Bar, and goodness knows it offers a better and safer livelihood. Others, including political leaders on both sides, have at various times sought to induce me to take to politics, going so far as to offer me ministries of my choice. Diplomats, recognizing the risk that journalists face in Sri Lanka, have offered me safe passage and right of residence in their countries. Whatever I may have been stuck for, I have not been stuck for choice. But there is a calling that is yet above high office, fame, lucre and security. It is the call of conscience.'

(*She looks up from the screen and repeats the last line.*)

'There is a calling that is yet above high office, fame, lucre and security. It is the call of conscience.'

That is the crux, isn't it? The bottomline. One's conscience. That line got right under my skin. The line that pushed me to make up my mind. I was going to be a member of your profession. I wanted to follow my conscience—to question, to investigate, to expose wrong-doing however powerful the wrong doer.

'What's wrong with you? Why are you choosing to be poor?' My mother.

'We thought this journalism school nonsense was timepass. You can't be serious.' My father.

'You're mad.' Friends, MBA batchmates, even distant relatives.

My world was against my decision. Your words were my support. Your words, not what our teachers had taught us. Your words inspired my decision.

(*She reads*)

'The free media serve as a mirror in which the public can see itself sans mascara and styling gel. From us you learn the state of your nation, especially its management by the people you elected to give your children a better future. Sometimes the image you see in that mirror is not pleasant. But while you may grumble in the privacy of your armchair, the journalists who hold the mirror up to you do so publicly and at great risk to themselves.'

You reminded me so much of Sir Thomas More. We had performed a play about him and King Henry VIII in college. I was part of the backstage team. I attended all the rehearsals. I knew the play backwards. I loved it. The king wants to marry a second time. That is against the Church. Sir Thomas won't support him. More has friends like yours. The Duke of Norfolk is one. At one point he says to More, 'Frankly, I don't know whether the marriage is lawful or not. But damn it, Thomas, look at those names . . . You know those men! Can't you do what I did, and come with us, for fellowship?'

More answers with gentle wit, 'And when we stand before God, and you are sent to Paradise for doing according to your conscience, and I am damned for not doing according to mine, will you come with me—for "fellowship"?'

(*She laughs*)

Sir Thomas More and the King were like you and Rajapaksa—old friends who had shared so much. You were fond of him too. Yet More stood up to the King as you stood up to the President, albeit not without deep regret.

(*Reads*)

'Mahinda, when you finally fought your way to the presidential nomination in 2005, nowhere were you welcomed more warmly than in this column. Indeed, we broke with a decade of tradition by referring to you throughout by your first name. So well known were your commitments to human rights and liberal values that we ushered you in like a breath of fresh air. Sadly, for all the dreams you had for our country in your younger days, in only three years you have reduced them to rubble. In the name of patriotism, you have trampled on human rights, nurtured unbridled corruption and squandered public money like no other president before you.'

Your words made no difference to your friend. Exactly five months and eleven days after he had you assassinated, President Rajapaksa delivered a victory address to Parliament, declaring Sri Lanka liberated from terrorism. That triumphant speech was not about the 40,000 civilians who were killed in the last stage of the war alone. The mothers who were brutally shot down, the children who were murdered. Were they terrorists too?

The President didn't care about them. You did. Because you cared about humanity.

(*Reads*)

'The LTTE are among the most ruthless and bloodthirsty organizations ever to have infested the planet. There is no gainsaying that it must be eradicated. But to do so by violating the rights of Tamil citizens, bombing and shooting them mercilessly is not only wrong but also shames the Sinhalese whose claim to being custodians of dhamma is forever called into question by this savagery.'

You saw the future clearly. You said that turning the Tamil people into second-class citizens, depriving them of all self-respect, would lead to 'strife for all eternity'. That is the phrase you used. That is exactly what happened. Your beloved Sri Lanka has become increasingly more intolerant. Sectarianism has risen to new heights. Years after your assassination, Buddhist mobs attacked businesses and homes belonging to minority Muslims. Why? Because, despite their clear majority, Sinhalese Buddhist nationalists have been stoking fears that minority groups, particularly the Muslims, are increasing in numbers and influence. It's an old strategy. Hitler used it. Our leaders have used it. Once nationalism gets going, it doesn't stop at one community or two. It rages on. The Sri Lankan civil war has reaped the harvest you predicted. 'Strife for all eternity'.

You too were inspired by someone as I was inspired by you. Your inspiration had lived and suffered in Nazi Germany. At first, he'd admired Hitler. Soon he recognized him for what he was. He did not end up dead like you but was incarcerated in concentration camps and very nearly executed. His name was Martin Niemöller. He wrote a poem that you read when you were a teenager. You say in your article that it 'stuck hauntingly' in your mind. It has come down to us too and is remembered every time people are cowed into silence by a vengeful, murderous, fascist state.

(*She reads. As she does so, a chorus of voices joins in.*)

First they came for the Jews and I did not speak out because I
was not a Jew.

Then they came for the Communists and I did not speak out
because I was not a Communist.

Then they came for the trade unionists and I did not speak out
because I was not a trade unionist.

Then they came for me and there was no one left to speak out
for me.

(*The voices stop. She gets up and paces the floor*)

I must write my letter of resignation now. I have written several drafts already. They have been full of righteous indignation, telling my newspaper how immoral it is and how suffocated and ashamed I feel working for it. Reading them over, I have laughed at this holier-than-thou me. I haven't yet proved how moral I am.

I now realize that there is such a thing as negative inspiration. My newspaper has provided it. A negative inspiration tells you where you don't want to be; what you don't want to do. That opens the door to discovering where you do want to be, what you do want to do. I said sorry to you, Lasantha Wickrematunge, at the beginning of this self-examination. I apologized to you because I had decided not only to quit this paper but the profession itself. I had been defending my decision on the grounds that you owned a newspaper. That gave you the freedom to speak truth to power. I do not own a newspaper. How can I pretend to have the freedom you had?

I admit now that this argument is lame. There is a whole world of opportunities out there that the Internet provides. Several news websites are fighting bravely for truth and justice. I will apply to them all till I win a space where I can perform my daily acts of conscience. They don't pay very much. But I ask myself: how much money do I really need to survive? Not much. So here goes.

(*She sits before her laptop and begins to type. Stops. Looks up and smiles. Reads.*)

'Dear sir, I am happy to say that I have decided to quit my job with you. Please accept my resignation. I would actually like to stop working from tomorrow. But I am prepared to fulfil my contractual obligation. I hereby give you one month's notice. Shakti.'

Yes. That's my name. Shakti.